THE KING IS COMING

PREPARING YOURSELF FOR THE RETURN OF CHRIST

BIBLE STUDY GUIDE | SIX SESSIONS

JOHN BEVERE

The King Is Coming Bible Study Guide

Published by HarperChristian Resources, 3950 Sparks Drive SE, Suite 101, Grand Rapids, MI 49546, USA. HarperChristian Resources is a registered trademark of HarperCollins Christian Publishing, Inc.

Requests for information should be addressed to customercare@harpercollins.com.

ISBN 978-0-310-17946-7 (softcover)
ISBN 978-0-310-17947-4 (ebook)

HarperChristian Resources titles may be purchased in bulk for church, business, fundraising, or ministry use. For information, please e-mail ResourceSpecialist@ChurchSource.com.

HarperCollins Publishers, Macken House, 39/40 Mayor Street Upper, Dublin 1, D01 C9W8, Ireland (https://www.harpercollins.com).

Art direction: Ron Huizinga
Cover Design: © 2025 HarperCollins Christian Publishing
Interior Design: Inside Out Design

First Printing February 2026

CONTENTS

SESSION 4: IS IT THE SEASON OF JESUS' RETURN?

SESSION 5: THE CATCHING AWAY OF HIS BRIDE

SESSION 6: HOW SHALL WE LIVE?

A NOTE FROM
JOHN BEVERE

For most of my forty years in ministry, I avoided the subject of the end times. I considered it too controversial, too confusing, and, at times, too easily abused. In the 1980s I watched well-meaning believers set dates, quit jobs, run up credit cards, and argue endlessly over who had the right timeline. I saw fear, pride, and division where there should have been hope and awe. Out of reaction, I decided, *I'm not touching that subject.*

But several years ago the Holy Spirit began tugging on my heart. I couldn't escape the sense that I was neglecting one of Scripture's most important truths: the return of Jesus Christ. So I started studying again, not through sensational headlines or speculation, but through the Word itself. What I discovered changed everything.

The more I focused on the promise of Jesus' return, the more passionate I became about living ready. Far from making me passive or withdrawn, prophecy awakened urgency, purity, and compassion in me. My love for Jesus grew deeper. My patience with people grew longer. My desire to reach the lost intensified. What I once dismissed as too divisive or complicated became the truth that brought clarity to everything else.

John writes in Revelation 1:3 that there is a blessing for those who read, hear, and obey the words of prophecy. In no other book of the Bible does God get that specific. He knew many of us would avoid this topic, so He attached a blessing to remind us that *the message matters.*

Prophecy isn't meant to produce fear but to anchor faith. It is intended to help us live this life more fully, serve more faithfully, love others more deeply, and shine more brightly until we see our King face-to-face. Prophecy reminds us that life is not random or chaotic but is moving toward the moment when the King returns to make all things new. Studying His coming makes us wiser, humbler, and more devoted in the present.

As you begin this journey, my prayer is that you will experience what I did—that the promise of Jesus' return will ignite love, purpose, and endurance in your heart. So let these sessions draw you closer to the One who is not only *coming soon* but who even now walks beside you. He is strengthening and preparing you for that day.

— **JOHN BEVERE**

HOW TO USE
THIS GUIDE

We live in a world that moves fast and worries move even faster. Global instability, natural disasters, cultural division, and personal uncertainties make it feel as if the ground is constantly shifting beneath our feet. But while the world changes, God does not. He has spoken clearly about what is ahead, and His plan is never uncertain.

The purpose of *The King Is Coming Bible Study* is not to stir up fear in you but to strengthen your faith. Prophecy is intended not to make you anxious but to give you confidence in the One who keeps His promises. As you go through this study, you will see that God's Word offers not confusion but clarity, not panic but peace, and not speculation but steady hope.

Before you begin, know that there are a few ways you can go through this material. You can experience this study with others in a group (such as a Bible study, Sunday school class, or other gathering), or you can go through the content on your own. Either way, the videos are available to view at any time by following the instructions provided with this study guide.

GROUP STUDY

Each of the sessions in this study guide is divided into two parts: (1) a group study section and (2) a personal study section. The group study section provides a basic framework on how to open your time together, get the most out of the video content, and discuss the key ideas that were presented in the teaching. Each session includes the following:

- **Welcome:** A short opening note about the topic of the session for you to read on your own before you meet as a group.

- **Open:** A few icebreaker questions to get you and your group members thinking about the topic and interacting with each other.
- **Watch:** An outline of the key points covered in each video teaching along with space for you to take notes as you watch each session.
- **Discuss:** Questions to help you and your group reflect on the teaching material presented and apply it to your lives.
- **Respond:** A short personal exercise to help reinforce the key ideas.
- **Pray:** A brief set of prompts to help you and your group take the next step in inviting God to be present and active in your lives.

If you are doing this study in a group, make sure you have your own copy of the study guide so you can write down your thoughts, responses, and reflections in the space provided—and so you have access to the videos via streaming. You will also want to have a copy of *The King Is Coming* book, as reading it alongside this guide will provide you with deeper insights. (See the notes at the beginning of each group session and personal study section on which chapters of the book you should read before the next group session.)

Finally, keep these points in mind:

- **Facilitation:** If you are doing this study in a group, you will want to appoint someone to serve as a facilitator. This person will be responsible for starting the video and keeping track of time during discussions and activities. If *you* have been chosen for this role, there are some resources in the back of this guide that can help you lead your group through the study.

- **Faithfulness:** Your group is a place where tremendous growth can happen as you reflect on the Bible, ask questions, and learn what God is doing in other people's lives. For this reason, be fully committed and attend each session so you can build trust and rapport with the other members.

- **Friendship:** The goal of any small group is to serve as a place where people can share, learn about God, and build friendships. So seek to make your group a safe place. Be honest about your thoughts and feelings, but also listen carefully to everyone else's thoughts, feelings, and opinions. Keep anything personal that your group members share in confidence so that you can create a community where people can heal, be challenged, and grow spiritually.

If you are going through this study on your own, read the opening Welcome section and reflect on the questions in the Open section. Watch the video and use the outline provided to help you take notes. Finally, personalize the questions and exercises in the Discuss and Respond sections. Close by recording any requests you want to pray about during the week.

PERSONAL STUDY

The personal study is for you to work through on your own during the week. Each exercise is designed to help you explore the key ideas you uncovered during your group time and delve into passages of Scripture that will help you apply those principles to your life. Go at your own pace, doing a little each day—or tackle the material all at once. Remember to spend a few moments in silence to listen to whatever God might be saying to you.

Note that if you are doing this study as part of a group, and you are unable to finish (or even start) these personal studies for the week, you should still plan to attend the group time. Be assured that you are still wanted and welcome even if you don't have your "homework" done. The group studies and personal studies are simply intended to be another tool to help you hear what God wants you to hear and how to apply what He is saying to your life. So, as you walk through each session, be attentive to how God is speaking. Let His Word take root within you, and let His promises become the steady ground beneath your faith.

WEEK 1 *at a glance*

THIS WEEK'S READING	Chapters 1-4 in *The King Is Coming*
GROUP MEETING	Read the Welcome and Open the group (page 2) Watch the video and take notes (pages 3-4) Discuss the questions that follow (page 5) Respond to the teaching and Pray (page 6)
PERSONAL STUDIES: **STUDY 1** **STUDY 2** **STUDY 3**	 "Hard to Miss" (pages 9-12) "Eyes That See" (pages 13-16) "On God's Clock" (pages 17-20)
CATCH UP AND CONNECT	Connect with someone in your group Complete any unfinished studies (page 21)
NEXT WEEK'S READING (BEFORE WEEK 2 GROUP MEETING)	Chapters 5-7 in *The King Is Coming*

SESSION ONE

WHY DON'T WE TALK ABOUT IT?

For prophecy never had its origin in the human will, but prophets, though human, spoke from God as they were carried along by the Holy Spirit.

2 PETER 1:21

WELCOME | READ ON YOUR OWN

We live in a time when talk of the end times often stirs confusion or silence. Many of us love Jesus deeply but quietly avoid the topic of His return. It can feel uncertain, mysterious, or even divisive. But the return of Jesus is not a side note in God's story; it is central to our hope.

God included prophecy in His Word not to make us fearful but to make us faithful. John wrote, "Blessed is the one who keeps the words of the prophecy written in this scroll" (Revelation 22:7). This blessing comes as we remember that the same Jesus who came once to redeem will come again to reign. When that truth stays before us, it gives strength to endure, wisdom to live well, and urgency to share the gospel.

We are called to live in awareness of God's "appointed time of the end" (Daniel 8:19). He determines the seasons of history, but He also gives insight to those who seek Him so they can live ready. Jesus rebuked the leaders of His day for knowing how to predict the weather but not knowing "how to interpret the present times" (Luke 12:56 NLT). We are called to stay alert—not fearful or fixated on dates, but responsive to what God is doing in our generation.

As you begin this study in God's Word, be sure to approach it with a spirit of anticipation, remembering that God invites His people to live with clear eyes and ready hearts. The King *is* coming. That truth should shape not only how you think about the future but also how you live today.

OPEN | 10 MINUTES

If you or any of your group members don't know each other, take a few minutes to introduce yourselves. Then discuss one or both of the following questions:

- Why did you decide to join this study? What do you hope to learn?

  — *or* —

- On a scale of 1 (low) to 10 (high), how would you rate your interest in biblical prophecy and the end times? Explain your response.

WATCH | 25 MINUTES

Watch the video for this session, which you can access through streaming (see the instructions provided with this guide). Below is an outline of the key points covered during the teaching. Record any key concepts that stand out to you.

OUTLINE

I. **Why do so many believers hesitate to talk about the second coming of Jesus?**
   A. Fear: some believers shy away because prophecy seems frightening or overwhelming to them.
   B. Confusion: others see it as too mysterious or difficult to understand.
   C. Division: debates over timing and interpretation have caused arguments.
   D. Disappointment: false predictions and failed dates have left many discouraged.

II. **Studying prophecy produces clear and lasting spiritual benefits.**
   A. God promises blessing to those who read, hear, and obey the prophetic Word (Revelation 1:3).
   B. Prophecy is a foundational doctrine of the church. It is included among the elementary teachings of the faith listed in Hebrews 6:1–2.
   C. Expectation of Christ's return keeps us urgent, guarding against spiritual laziness and distraction.
   D. Living with the hope of Jesus' return purifies us, shaping our character and drawing us closer to the holiness of Christ (1 John 3:2–3).

III. **Understanding prophecy equips us to live faithfully in the present.**
   A. Understanding biblical prophecy keeps our focus on God's larger story so we don't get lost in daily distractions.
   B. Biblical prophecy reminds us that history is moving toward fulfillment, not drifting without purpose.
   C. It motivates us to share the gospel with urgency while there is still time.

IV. **God calls His people to respond with reverence, expectancy, and readiness.**
   A. Luke tells the story of a man named Simeon who was "righteous and devout and was eagerly waiting for the Messiah to come and rescue Israel" (2:25 NLT).
   B. Because Simeon feared God and listened to the Spirit, he recognized Jesus when others did not.
   C. We are called to live in a similar posture of remaining alert to God's purposes, confident that His promises will be fulfilled.

NOTES

DISCUSS | 35 MINUTES

Discuss what you just watched by answering the following questions.

1. When it comes to considering what the Bible says about what will happen as we approach the end times, it often seems that different denominations, churches, pastors, ministry leaders, and individual believers have different visions of "what happens next." What have you been taught about the next steps in God's plan for the future?

2. In this session, you heard that studying the return of Jesus brings blessings to your life, strengthens your foundation, renews your urgency, and purifies your heart. Which of these effects stands out to you most? Why?

3. Invite someone to read aloud Matthew 24:42–44. Jesus told His followers to "keep watch" and "be ready" because His return will come unexpectedly. What does staying spiritually alert look like in everyday life?

4. Ask someone to read 2 Peter 3:11–12 to the group. Peter connects the promise of Jesus' return with living "holy and godly lives." How does focusing on the coming of the Lord reshape your goals, attitudes, or priorities?

5. The stories of Simeon and Anna remind us that God honors those who live watchfully and faithfully. How has this session deepened your understanding of why the return of Christ is essential to your faith? What difference does that make in how you live with hope today?

RESPOND | 10 MINUTES

The return of Jesus is meant to steady your heart. When you remember that God will fulfill His promises in His perfect time, you can live with quiet confidence and hope. Take a few minutes to read the passage below and reflect on what it means to stay anchored in that assurance.

> For the grace of God has appeared that offers salvation to all people. It teaches us to say "No" to ungodliness and worldly passions, and to live self-controlled, upright and godly lives in this present age, while we wait for the blessed hope—the appearing of the glory of our great God and Savior, Jesus Christ.
>
> **TITUS 2:11–13**

How does this passage connect grace and holiness with our hope in Jesus' return? What might it look like for that "blessed hope" to shape your daily choices?

Look at the verbs in this passage . . . words like *teaches, say no, live,* and *wait.* Which of these feels the most challenging or encouraging to you right now? Why?

PRAY | 10 MINUTES

As you close this session, take time to thank God for giving you His Word and the promise of Christ's return. Acknowledge His control over history, from the beginning of creation to the day of Jesus' appearing. Ask Him to help you live with hope and readiness, staying watchful for His purposes in your life and in the world. Pray that He would purify your heart, strengthen your faith, and guide you with wisdom as you continue through this study.

SESSION ONE

PERSONAL STUDY

This week, you explored why many Christians avoid talking about prophecy and how the Bible itself urges us to engage with it. You saw that God promises blessing to those who read and obey His prophetic Word and that studying the second coming strengthens your foundation, stirs urgency, and purifies your heart. You also learned from the example of Simeon that living in anticipation of Christ's coming requires righteousness, devotion, and attentiveness to God's timing. The personal exercises for this week will help you dive deeper into these topics. As you work through them, write down your responses to the questions, as you will be given a few minutes to share your insights if you are doing this study with a group. If you are reading *The King Is Coming,* first review the introduction and chapters 1–4 of the book.

They will say, "What happened to
the promise that Jesus is
coming again? From before the
times of our ancestors,
everything has remained the same
since the world was first created."

2 PETER 3:4 NLT

STUDY 1

HARD TO MISS

If something is mentioned once in Scripture, it's worth noticing. If it's mentioned repeatedly, it's worth remembering. But if it's mentioned hundreds of times, it's worth taking to heart.

Jesus' second coming isn't a minor theme but is one of the Bible's most emphasized truths. It appears 318 times in the New Testament alone—roughly one out of every thirty verses—which makes it hard to miss. The early church couldn't stop talking about it, teaching about it, and looking forward to it. For them, hope in Christ's return wasn't abstract theology but the very air they breathed.

So, if that was their perspective, why do so many Christians avoid the topic today? Somewhere along the way, the conversation about Jesus' return became cluttered by fear, arguments, and disappointment. But the sheer frequency of the teaching tells us something important: God didn't include it to confuse us. He repeated it so we wouldn't forget it.

The message of Jesus' return grounds us in purpose. It reminds us that life is moving toward a certain conclusion—one planned by a faithful God. The same Lord who came once to redeem will come again to restore. Each reference, each promise, is a reminder that history is not drifting but being directed.

So if God gave this much attention to the second coming, maybe we should too. Not to predict dates or speculate on details but to let the truth shape how we live, love, and wait. Every reminder of His return is an invitation to hope and remain ready for the day we finally see Him face-to-face.

1. Read Matthew 24:32–35. List two temporary things Jesus says will "pass away" (verse 35) and two things that will last.

Things that will pass away	Things that last forever
❶	
❷	

2. How should knowing what will endure reshape your priorities today?

Peter writes, "Most importantly, I want to remind you that in the last days scoffers will come" (2 Peter 3:3 NLT). Notice that he begins this warning with the words "most importantly." Stop and ponder this for a moment. This is an attention grabber! Why does Peter single out the return of Jesus over the numerous other truths spoken of in the Word of God? Why doesn't he write this regarding the baptism of the Holy Spirit, the gifts of the Holy Spirit, praying in tongues, women in ministry, laying on of hands, or other current controversial topics? Why does Peter single out the second coming by attaching "most importantly" to it? Could it be it's a major foundational teaching of the Lord Jesus Christ, and our great adversary, the devil, knows the powerful potential of accurately studying and pondering it, and therefore seeks to discredit it?[1]

3. How might recognizing the enemy's effort to discredit the second coming change the way you approach studying prophecy or talking about Jesus' return with others?

4. Jesus' return is mentioned 318 times in the New Testament. Why might God have chosen to repeat this truth so often? What does repetition reveal about its importance to Him?

Read what is stated at the very beginning of the final book of the Bible: "God blesses the one who *reads* the words of this prophecy to the church, and he blesses all who *listen to* its message and obey what it says, for the time is near" (Revelation 1:3 NLT, emphasis added). There is a called out specific blessing connected with *reading, listening to,* and *obeying* the prophetic Word of God! This promise isn't articulated or written so specifically in any other book of the Bible. Why? Could one reason be the foreknowledge of God—that He foresaw end time teaching would be avoided, and even mocked, more so than any other doctrine in our time?[2]

5. Read Psalm 119:17–19. What might it look like for you to approach prophecy in the Bible with the prayer, "Open my eyes to see the wonderful truths in your instructions" (verse 18 NLT)?

How could that particular posture change the way you read God's promises about the future?

STUDY 2

EYES THAT SEE

When Jesus came to earth, the people who recognized Him as the Messiah weren't the scholars, priests, or rulers. They were ordinary people whose hearts were tuned to God's Spirit. Simeon and Anna had spent years waiting in the temple, holding on to God's promises when others had grown weary. Because they listened and stayed near, they saw what others missed.

This same contrast exists today. Some people know a great deal about the Bible but miss its heart. Others, like Simeon and Anna, may not have all the answers but walk so closely with God that when He moves, they recognize it instantly. Jesus said, "Blessed are your eyes because they see, and your ears because they hear" (Matthew 13:16). Seeing clearly begins with a humble heart and a willingness to wait on God's timing.

The same Spirit who revealed Jesus to Simeon and Anna continues to open eyes today. When you stay close to God in worship, obedience, and prayer, you develop a spiritual sensitivity that cuts through distraction and confusion—and you are not caught off guard. Prophecy therefore isn't meant to make you anxious, or even curious, but to keep you close to God. He doesn't want you to analyze headlines but to align your heart. The more time you spend in His presence, the more easily you will recognize His fingerprints in the world.

Ask yourself: *Am I recognizing how Jesus is at work now—in the moments leading up to His return? Am I seeing His faithfulness in the waiting, His mercy in the delay, His purpose in the process?* Simeon and Anna remind us that those who walk closely with God won't miss what He is doing. Spiritual vision isn't about seeing with your eyes but about seeing with your heart.

1. Read Luke 2:25–32. Simeon recognized Jesus because he was in tune with the Holy Spirit. On a scale of 1 to 10, how closely do you feel you are listening for God's direction right now?

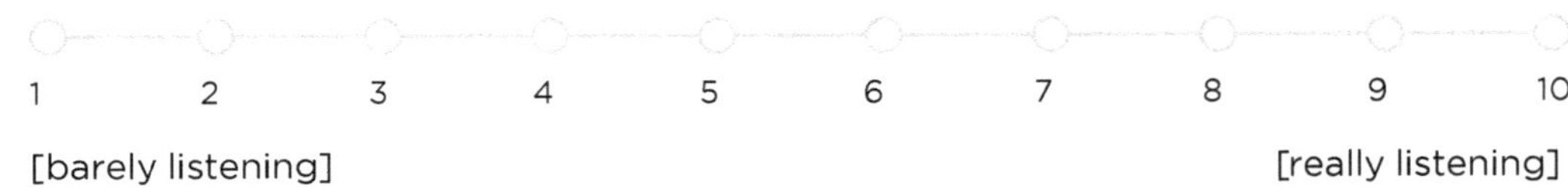

What practical step could move you one point higher on that scale this week?

2. Read Matthew 13:16–17. Jesus said many longed to see what His followers saw but didn't. What distractions or assumptions make it hard to see what God is doing around you today?

Luke identifies Simeon as being *devout.* It's the Greek word *eulabḗs,* meaning "one who had taken seriously God's promises and God's Word."[3] Simeon didn't avoid or shrug off the prophetic words of God but read, listened to, meditated on, and, most importantly, prayed about them. He didn't have the attitude, *When Messiah comes, He will just do it. Why should I give any attention to this matter?* This Greek word *eulabḗs* pertains "to being reverent toward God."[4] It describes one who lives in the holy fear of God. Simeon held firmly to this virtue, and it enlightened him with insight that others who lacked it didn't possess (see Proverbs 8:13–14).[5]

3. How does taking God's Word seriously, as Simeon did, influence the way you listen for His direction or respond to what He reveals in Scripture?

4. Read Proverbs 9:10–12. How does "the fear of the Lord" (verse 10) help you see life, faith, and the future with clearer perspective?

In the first century, not too different from our twenty-first-century church, there were factions of religious groups in Israel—the Pharisees, Sadducees, Essenes, and Scribes, to name just a few. (We didn't know much about the Essenes until the discovery of the Dead Sea Scrolls. We owe a debt of gratitude for their stewardship of the early writings. They were the group of devout followers who hid the sacred writings in the caves of Qumran.)

Sadly, many leaders were adversarial to the Creator who came as a humble Servant. Though they professed loyalty to Almighty God and the writings of the Law and Prophets, their hearts were proud, corrupt, and unteachable, thus blinding them to the arrival of the lowly King.

At the same time, there were others who did anticipate the time and whereabouts of His arrival. Simply put, they recognized Him. How did they know, while most didn't? The simple answer lies in their sensitivity to the Spirit of God and attention given to the writings of the Old Testament, especially the Prophets. Their hunger for God created in them an awareness of the times. What advantage was that? They knew what to do, whether it was waiting, speaking, or a specific action.[6]

5. What helps you to stay teachable and spiritually aware in a world that often rewards pride and self-reliance? How will you pursue these things this week?

STUDY 3

ON GOD'S CLOCK

Most of us like to think we're in charge of our schedule. We make plans, set goals, and measure progress by our calendars. Yet *God's* timeline runs much deeper than our own. "He changes times and seasons" (Daniel 2:21). This truth humbles us, because it means no matter how organized or determined we are, the real movement of life belongs to Him.

Jesus told the Pharisees that they could predict the weather but they had failed to interpret the "present time" (Luke 12:56). They had missed what God was doing because their expectations didn't match His plan. Knowing the times and seasons isn't about predicting dates; it's about recognizing God's hand in motion and adjusting our hearts accordingly.

Daniel modeled this beautifully. When he realized through Jeremiah's writings that Israel's captivity would last seventy years (see Jeremiah 25:11–12), he didn't sit back in resignation. He sought the Lord with fasting and prayer (Daniel 9:2–3). His awareness moved him to action. That's the kind of sensitivity God desires in us: not curiosity but cooperation.

If we pay attention, the Spirit often whispers that one season is closing and another is beginning. Our job is to listen, trust, and prepare. The believer who learns to move in rhythm with God's timing avoids unnecessary striving and stays aligned with His will.

The prophetic Word doesn't just tell us what is coming; it trains us to live alert and faithful *right now.* God isn't asking us to predict the future but to stay attuned to His presence in the present. When we live aware of His timing, we walk with peace instead of pressure, confident that He is preparing us for what He has already prepared.

1. Read Ecclesiastes 3:1–8. Which of the following words best describes the season you feel you're in right now? (Circle all that apply.)

Planting	Pruning	Waiting
Harvesting	Restoring	Rebuilding

How does knowing that *God has appointed this time* change how you move through it?

2. Read Daniel 2:19–23. Daniel acknowledged that God "changes times and seasons" (verse 21). In your life, what evidence do you see that God is guiding your circumstances? Write one or two examples below.

God may choose to hide appointed times or seasons, and in other situations, He desires for us to know them. Just before ascending to heaven, Jesus said to His disciples, "It is not for you to know times or seasons which the Father has put in His own authority" (Acts 1:7 NKJV). Yet, on the contrary, God spoke through the prophet Jeremiah, "You will be in Babylon for seventy years. But then I will come and do for you all the good things I have promised, and I will bring you home again" (Jeremiah 29:10 NLT). These are not contradictions; rather, with some appointed times awareness is granted, and with others, they are kept secret. Our responsibility is to seek God. If He chooses to reveal the time or season, it can be in a general sense, or it can be specific.[7]

3. What does it look like for you to seek God when He hasn't revealed the timing of something for which you have been praying? How might trusting His authority over the times and seasons change your posture while you wait?

4. Read Romans 13:11–12. Paul says the hour has already come to "wake up from your slumber" (verse 11). Which of the following areas of your faith most needs fresh alertness? (Circle the one that best applies.)

your prayer life | your relationships | your priorities | your daily obedience

How can prophecy help keep you awake and focused in the area you identified?

We as believers get ourselves into trouble when we shout what God whispers and we whisper what He shouts. Let me give you an example. Jesus, more than once, rebuked the Pharisees for getting the two backward. These leaders were sticklers for paying tithes and would even pay 10 percent of their garden herbs, yet they neglected the "weightier matters" of the Word of God, such as justice, mercy, and faith (Matthew 23:23). So, clearly, there are more important matters in Scripture.[8]

---

5. What are some ways you might be giving attention to the "lesser things" in your spiritual life while overlooking the "weightier ones" that God values most? How can studying prophecy help you keep those priorities in balance?

CATCH UP AND CONNECT

Consider connecting with a fellow group member sometime this week to discuss some of your key insights from this session. Use any of the following prompts to help guide your discussion.

- What did you find most meaningful from this session, whether in the video teaching or your personal study time? Why did that part stand out to you?
- What keeps people today from talking about Jesus' return? What emotions (positive or negative) surface when the topic of prophecy comes up?
- Studying prophecy brings blessing, urgency, and purity. Which of those three feels the most needed in your life right now? Why?
- How has this session reshaped your understanding of why God includes so much prophecy in the Bible?
- As you look ahead to the next session, what question do you have, or what are you most curious about, that you hope to explore?

Use this time to go back and complete any of the study and reflection questions from previous days that you weren't able to finish. Make a note below of any revelations you've had and reflect on any growth or personal insights you've gained.

NEXT WEEK'S READING: Chapters 5–7 in *The King Is Coming*

WEEK 2 *at a glance*

THIS WEEK'S READING	Chapters 5–7 in *The King Is Coming*
GROUP MEETING	Read the Welcome and Open the group (page 24) Watch the video and take notes (pages 25–26) Discuss the questions that follow (page 27) Respond to the teaching and Pray (page 28)
PERSONAL STUDIES: **STUDY 1** **STUDY 2** **STUDY 3**	 "Born for More" (pages 31–34) "Love That Stays" (pages 35–38) "Forged to Reign" (pages 39–42)
CATCH UP AND CONNECT	Connect with someone in your group Complete any unfinished studies (page 43)
NEXT WEEK'S READING (BEFORE WEEK 3 GROUP MEETING)	Chapters 8–10 in *The King Is Coming*

SESSION TWO

THE DIVINE MASTER PLAN

"I am God, and there is no other;
I am God, and there is none like me. I make
known the end from the beginning, from
ancient times, what is still to come."

ISAIAH 46:9–10

WELCOME | READ ON YOUR OWN

For us to fully understand what lies ahead, we first need to step back and look at God's divine master plan. Long before the first sunrise, He had already chosen to make Himself known through creation, redemption, and relationship. God's plan was to form a family that would share in His glory and reign with Him forever. Nothing about the cross or the return of Christ is a reaction to chaos. It is the unfolding of a divine master plan set in motion from eternity past.

The cross wasn't simply the rescue of humanity. It was the revelation of a heart willing to suffer for what it loves. Every covenant, prophetic promise, and act of redemption reveals God's relentless desire to restore what was lost. Understanding prophecy is about understanding who God is and how He works. When we see His timing and His ways, we stop living in panic and start living in partnership with Him.

As you go through this session, you will reflect on those moments in life when obedience feels costly and surrender feels heavy. But even those seasons are part of God's refining work. Just as Christ learned obedience through what He suffered, so God uses hardship to deepen intimacy with His people. Your pain is not wasted when it's joined to His purpose. Remember, prophecy is *revelation*. It reveals the heart of a Father who has never stopped pursuing His family and who will one day complete the story He started before time began.

OPEN | 10 MINUTES

If you or any of your group members don't know each other, take a few minutes to introduce yourselves. Then discuss one or both of the following questions:

- What is something that spoke to you in last week's personal study that you would like to share with the group?

  — *or* —

- How does the fact that God has a master plan affect how you see your own life story—especially the times that have felt delayed or difficult?

WATCH | 25 MINUTES

Now watch the video for this session. Below is an outline of the key points covered during the teaching. Record any key concepts that stand out to you.

OUTLINE

I. **Why does prophetic vision matter?**
   A. Without prophetic vision, people lose restraint and drift toward worldliness (Proverbs 29:18).
   B. Purpose changes perspective. What seems pointless makes sense when we see the bigger plan.
   C. When we lack understanding of God's eternal purpose and divine master plan, the second coming feels distant and irrelevant.

II. **God's eternal purpose existed before time began.**
   A. Before creation, the Father, Son, and Spirit designed a redemptive plan. Jesus would serve as the Lamb slain from the foundation of the world (Revelation 13:8).
   B. Humanity was created to reflect God's image and share His rule, but sin fractured that purpose and handed the dominion over to Satan.
   C. The cross was not a reaction to sin but the revelation of God's love and sovereignty.
   D. The Bible reveals God's continuous plan for restoring His family and reclaiming His kingdom.

III. **There is power and purpose in suffering.**
   A. Just as Christ learned obedience through suffering, so believers are refined through hardship.
   B. Obedience under pressure reveals our faith and deepens our intimacy with God.
   C. Shared suffering creates loyalty between the bride and the Bridegroom.

IV. **There is a love story at the center of prophecy.**
   A. Prophecy is not primarily about timelines. It is about a relationship that began before time began and will culminate in perfect union.
   B. God's eternal plan reveals His heart to dwell with His people in love, not distance.
   C. The second coming is the fulfillment of that love story, when the bride—purified through faith and perseverance—is united with her King.
   D. Prophecy points to this moment when heaven and earth join under Jesus' reign.

NOTES

DISCUSS | 35 MINUTES

Discuss what you just watched by answering the following questions.

1. "Where there is no revelation, people cast off restraint" (Proverbs 29:18). What insights did you gain in this week's teaching about God's divine master plan? How can those insights help you stay focused and vigilant about pursuing the things of God?

2. Even before the world was formed, God the Father knew that humans would sin and turn themselves over to the devil. What does it mean to you that Jesus' offer to go to the cross and rescue humanity was not a reaction but part of God's plan from the beginning?

3. Invite someone to read Isaiah 50:6 and 52:14. Before Jesus went to the cross, He was moved five different times and beaten beyond recognition, fulfilling the prophetic words of these passages. How does seeing the precision of these prophecies and the extent of Jesus' suffering deepen your understanding of both obedience and love in your relationship with God? In what ways does it give you greater confidence in other biblical prophecies?

4. Ask someone to read aloud Romans 8:17, and then ask another person in the group to summarize it in their own words. How does this perspective challenge modern ideas of comfort, success, or prosperity in the Christian life?

5. The second coming of Jesus is more than just a global event. It's the moment when Christ, the Groom, will be united with His bride, the church. How does viewing prophecy through that lens affect the way you live now? What would it look like to prepare for Jesus' return with the same devotion and anticipation as someone preparing for a wedding?

RESPOND | 10 MINUTES

Prophecy and the crucifixion are inseparable. Long before Jesus went to the cross, the prophets spoke of it in detail, telling where it would happen, how He would suffer, and what it would accomplish. Every strike, every insult, and every nail fulfilled a plan written centuries earlier. Yet the cross was not the end of the story but the center point of a plan that stretches from eternity past to eternity future. It was a demonstration of prophecy fulfilled.

> But he was pierced for our transgressions, he was crushed for our iniquities; the punishment that brought us peace was on him, and by his wounds we are healed.
>
> **ISAIAH 53:5**

Take a moment to really consider what Jesus did for you by going to the cross. How does it impact you to know that He agreed to suffer and die for you *knowing* that you would sin and rebel against Him? What does this say about His love for you?

What does this say about Jesus' love for you when it comes to His second coming? How does the reality of His return give you confidence to live faithfully for Him today?

PRAY | 10 MINUTES

As you close this session, thank God for being a loving heavenly Father who keeps every promise—from the ones fulfilled at the cross to the ones still unfolding in your lifetime. Ask Him to help you see your place not just as a spectator in His story but as someone called to live with purpose and anticipation. Pray that your faith would stay steady when life feels uncertain and that your hope in Jesus' return would shape how you work, love, and lead every day.

SESSION TWO

PERSONAL STUDY

Life moves fast, and most days it's easy to forget that God's story is still unfolding you. Between home, hobbies, work, relationships, and everyday responsibilities, eternity can feel far away. However, as you explored during this week's group time, God's plan isn't distant but is already in motion—and you are part of it. Long before you took your first breath, God wrote a plan of redemption that would reveal His love through the cross and prove His power through prophecy. Both remind you that life isn't random but is directed by a faithful God who finishes what He starts. The personal exercises for this week will help you dive deeper into these topics. As you work through them, write down your responses to the questions, as you will be given a few minutes to share your insights if you are doing this study with a group. If you are reading *The King Is Coming*, first review chapters 5–7 of the book.

For I am jealous for you
with the jealousy of God himself.
I promised you as a pure bride to
one husband—Christ.

2 CORINTHIANS 11:2 NLT

STUDY 1

BORN FOR MORE

Many of us spend our lives chasing more . . . more achievement, more connection, more meaning. But God's idea of "more" has always been deeper than what we can reach on our own. From the start, He designed us to live as heirs of His kingdom—not as spectators on the sidelines but as sons and daughters with full access to His presence and purpose.

You weren't an afterthought in God's plan. You were written into it from the start. Long before creation, God had already mapped out the story of redemption. Prophecy wasn't added later to make sense of the plan; it was the way God announced it in advance, piece by piece, so His people would recognize His hand in every generation. The cross wasn't damage control or a course correction but the centerpiece of His divine plan for humankind.

God's goal was never to rule over creation by Himself but to share that rule with a family who would love Him freely. The prophets foretold it, Jesus fulfilled it, and one day every word will reach its completion when He returns. You were born into that unfolding story—a story that spans from creation to eternity, written by a God who never improvises.

Paul wrote, "Now if we are children, then we are heirs—heirs of God and co-heirs with Christ" (Romans 8:17). You're not just *waiting* for heaven; you're being *trained* for it. Every challenge, every moment of faithfulness, and every act of obedience is shaping you for your future inheritance. God's timeline is precise, and His promises are already in motion. So when life feels ordinary or aimless, remember that *you were born for more.* You were born to carry the image of Jesus into this world and to live like someone who knows how the story ends.

1. Circle which of the following words best describes how you currently see yourself in God's plan.

Included Developing Overlooked Ready Uncertain

What would help you move closer to truly believing you were born for more?

2. Prophecy reveals that the promises of God found their fulfillment in Jesus and point toward His return. Which of God's promises feels hardest for you to believe right now? What step could help you anchor your faith more deeply in His proven track record?

> Imagine a global ruler—a king who is the wealthiest, wisest, and most noble in all the world, one who cannot be matched or defeated. He travels to one of his territories in the outer realm and during the visit decides to tour one of the most impoverished communities, a slum. In the process, he beholds an utterly poor and helpless young man (or woman) and is moved with empathy and compassion. Suddenly, to the surprise of his attendants and soldiers, he chooses to take this destitute homeless young person into his family, and not just to adopt but to make him (or her) heir to all he owns. . . . This is merely a very weak example of what God has done for us.[9]

3. Read Ephesians 1:18–21. What does Paul want you to be enlightened to know? What does he reveal about your inheritance if you are a follower of Christ?

4. Read Romans 8:14–17. What does being an heir of God mean for your choices, your attitude at work or home, and your sense of purpose today?

God makes a bold challenge: "Let them tell us what the future holds . . . tell us what will occur in the days ahead. Then we will know you are gods" (Isaiah 41:22–23 NLT). Have there been a few individuals who've accurately predicted future events by chance? Of course. Have there been familiar spirits who have heard things from God's throne, which He permitted, and subsequently revealed this knowledge to a few humans? Again, yes. However, He's the only One who truly foretells and controls the future. God has a master plan that was formulated before time began, and in this regard He declares: "I will accomplish all my purpose" (Isaiah 46:10 ESV).[10]

5. Read God's words to His people in Isaiah 46:10–13. What does this passage say about the certainty of God's plans coming to pass?

What should this prophecy compel the "stubborn-hearted" (verse 12) to do?

STUDY 2

LOVE THAT STAYS

God kept His master plan—the one He made "for our ultimate glory" (1 Corinthians 2:7 NLT)—a secret for *thousands* of years. He knew if it leaked out, the dark rulers of this world wouldn't have played into it so perfectly. So, when Jesus came into this world—teaching truth that set people free—He was misunderstood, misrepresented, and resisted at nearly every turn. He was lied about, labeled a heretic, and plotted against by the very people He came to save.

Yet Jesus' love remained steady through every insult and rejection. As the author of Hebrews states, "For the joy set before him he endured the cross" (12:2). Jesus knew *exactly* what awaited Him, but He kept walking toward the cross because of the joy in knowing He was fulfilling God's plan. The agony He faced wasn't a surprise—it was the cost of His love.

Every prophecy about Jesus' suffering is a reminder that none of it was accidental. And the resolve Jesus demonstrated reveals something vital about God's plan: *It doesn't fall apart when life feels chaotic.* If prophecy could hold true in the darkest moment of history, then it certainly can hold true in the darkest moments of your history.

Jesus' endurance isn't just something to admire but something to model. He stayed faithful when life got loud, misunderstood, and costly. His strength is available to you. When your schedule feels relentless and faith feels like one more thing to do, you can remember the bigger picture: *Your life has purpose beyond the pace.* Jesus' steady love empowers you to live and speak with hope in every moment of every day. His story reminds you that what feels small or unseen might be the very place God is revealing His glory through you.

1. On a scale of 1 to 10, how steady is your faith when life feels unpredictable?

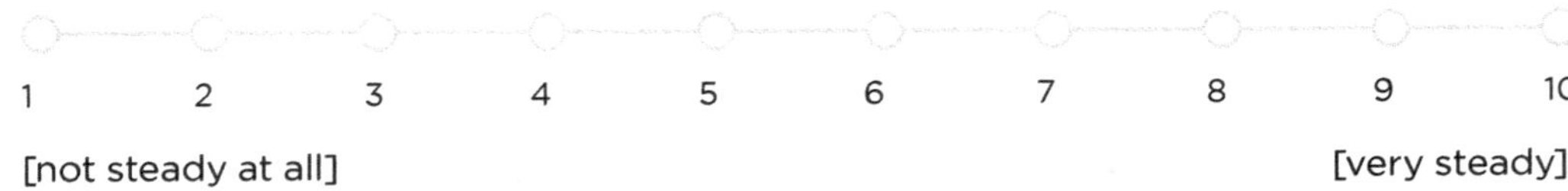

[not steady at all] [very steady]

What makes it especially difficult to trust that God's plan is still unfolding when you can't see how?

Imagine hiding a wonderful secret from those you love—a plan you've devised for their best interest. You'd give them clues along the way, but during this long stretch of time you'd refrain from sharing your magnificent strategy with the very ones for whom it's intended. Not an easy thing to do, yet the Lord did exactly this! God kept His grandest plan, the one He made "for our ultimate glory" (1 Corinthians 2:7 NLT) a secret, not just for decades or centuries but for thousands of years. He knew if it leaked out, the dark rulers of this world wouldn't have played into it so perfectly.[11]

2. Read 1 Corinthians 2:6–8. What is the "mystery that has been hidden" (verse 7) that Paul describes? Why did God choose to keep His plans for Jesus' death on the cross a secret?

3. Read Philippians 2:5–8. In this passage, Paul describes how Jesus made Himself nothing by taking on the nature of a servant. What does Jesus' humility in choosing the cross teach you about how to approach power, success, or recognition in your own life?

Where might God be inviting you to serve quietly and trust that He sees what others might not?

Why would Jesus undergo such agony and sacrifice to rescue us when we were totally at fault, when we betrayed Him? We read: "Because of the joy awaiting him, he endured the cross" (Hebrews 12:2 NLT).

He saw something that kept Him going. It was the prophetic vision of a faithful bride! He foresaw beautiful, intimate companionship, deep love, and trust between Himself and His bride in the ages to come. He saw the wedding and the celebration of our lives being united as one. He saw us reigning together for the rest of eternity.

His devotion to us is affirmed by His suffering for us, and our dedication to Him would be affirmed in our suffering for Him.[12]

---

4. Read Hebrews 12:1–3. What does it mean to run the "race marked out for us" (verse 1)? How does keeping our focus on Jesus enable us to run that race with endurance?

5. Paul wrote that Jesus died for us "while we were still sinners" (Romans 5:8). What does this reveal about Jesus' love for you? How does this compel you to love others like Jesus loves?

STUDY 3

FORGED TO REIGN

"Let us be glad and rejoice, and let us give honor to him. For the time has come for the wedding feast of the Lamb, and his bride has prepared herself" (Revelation 19:7 NLT). All of prophecy is moving toward one defining event: the return of Jesus, when heaven and earth will be made whole. But John's vision of the bride getting ready for her groom isn't just about the end of time but also about the process God is using right now to prepare our hearts.

The author of Hebrews states that God the Father, "in bringing many sons and daughters to glory," found it fitting to make Jesus "the pioneer" of our salvation "through what he suffered" (2:10). Jesus didn't lead from a distance; He led by walking through pain first. Every wound He bore became a bridge that draws us closer to Him. And in following Him, we discover that the road to intimacy is often paved with endurance.

Even human experience reflects this truth. Deep bonds are not formed in comfort but in difficulty. Soldiers who share battles, friends who survive crises, families who endure loss . . . they all come out closer to each other because they have suffered together. In the same way, we are joined to Christ through shared struggle. When we choose faith in hardship, we deepen our connection with the One who has already endured it all for us.

Paul wrote, "If we endure, we will also reign with him" (2 Timothy 2:12). The fire you face today is not *punishment* but *refinement*. God is shaping a bride who will reflect His Son. One day, all the pain will give way to joy at the wedding feast of the Lamb. But until then, every hardship is an invitation to walk more closely with your Lord, share His endurance, and love Him more deeply because of what you've come through together.

1. Read 1 Peter 4:12–14. What reasons did Peter give as to why you can rejoice when a "fiery ordeal" (verse 12) comes your way because of your faith in Christ?

2. How could this passage reframe the way you see seasons of struggle? What would it mean to view your pain as participation in something sacred rather than as punishment?

Studies have shown mutual suffering makes the connection of love deep.[13] Jesus (the pioneer) suffered first for us, but it's followed by His bride's willingness to suffer for Him, which fosters in us a deeper bond for Him! This seems ludicrous to the Western mindset, but let's go to Scripture for confirmation. The apostle Paul writes that he counts all his accomplishments and accolades as garbage so that he can press on to the highest calling: "I want to know Christ. . . . I want to suffer with him, sharing in his death" (Philippians 3:10 NLT). . . . For what purpose does Paul want to suffer with Jesus? The answer is to know Him more deeply—to have a stronger connection with Him.[14]

3. Read Philippians 3:10–12. What kind of association does Paul say that he wants to have with Christ? What is his motivation and end goal in this pursuit?

4. James wrote, "Blessed is the one who perseveres under trial because, having stood the test, that person will receive the crown of life" (1:12). What are some of the "crown moments" that God has used to show His faithfulness to you?

♛ ______________________________

____

♛ ______________________________

____

♛ ______________________________

____

♛ ______________________________

____

True biblical suffering is simply this: We live in a fallen world, one that opposes the truth of God—the ways of His kingdom. A true believer chooses to obey God's Word in the face of any resistant force. It can come from a temptation, a trial, or persecution for our faith. The fruit is we will live "no longer for human passions [*whether our own or others'*] but for the will of God" (1 Peter 4:2 ESV).

Stop and ponder the wonder of God's master plan. He chose to suffer from a world that hates Him. In doing so, He would pay the price needed to free His bride from sin and death, but also in the process would bond deeply with her. She in turn would deeply bond with Him through the sufferings she'd face in a very perverse and cruel world. This strong bond would intensify the desire He would have to be reunited with her and she with Him. The second coming isn't just an event, *it is the uniting of two lovers*, a Groom and bride-to-be who deeply long for each other. Oh, how marvelous is the wisdom of God![15]

5. How does seeing the second coming as the reunion of two lovers—Christ and His bride—change how you think about your relationship with Jesus today?

CATCH UP AND CONNECT

Consider connecting with a fellow group member sometime this week to discuss some of your key insights from this session. Use any of the following prompts to help guide your discussion.

- What part of this week's teaching or personal study helped you see Jesus in a new way? Why did that insight feel meaningful to you?
- Prophecy reminds us that God's plan is precise, even when life feels uncertain. How does seeing His faithfulness through fulfilled prophecy encourage you to trust Him with what is still ahead?
- Suffering can deepen our bond with Christ. Can you think of a season in your life when difficulty led you to experience God's presence more closely?
- Jesus is the "pioneer" of our salvation, showing us the way through hardship to glory. How does His example comfort you in your current season?
- Looking ahead, what do you most hope to understand more deeply about God's plan for His people and His return?

Use this time to go back and complete any of the study and reflection questions from previous days that you weren't able to finish. Make a note below of any revelations you've had and reflect on any growth or personal insights you've gained.

NEXT WEEK'S READING: **Chapters 8–10 in *The King Is Coming***

WEEK 3 *at a glance*

THIS WEEK'S READING	Chapters 8–10 in *The King Is Coming*
GROUP MEETING	Read the Welcome and Open the group (page 46) Watch the video and take notes (pages 47–48) Discuss the questions that follow (page 49) Respond to the teaching and Pray (page 50)
PERSONAL STUDIES: **STUDY 1** **STUDY 2** **STUDY 3**	 "Built on Trust" (pages 53–56) "Right on Time" (pages 57–60) "Ready or Not" (pages 61–64)
CATCH UP AND CONNECT	Connect with someone in your group Complete any unfinished studies (page 65)
NEXT WEEK'S READING (BEFORE WEEK 4 GROUP MEETING)	Chapters 11–13 in *The King Is Coming*

SESSION THREE

THE ANCIENT JEWISH WEDDING

"My Father's house has many rooms; if that were not so, would I have told you that I am going there to prepare a place for you? And if I go and prepare a place for you, I will come back and take you to be with me that you also may be where I am."

JOHN 14:2-3

WELCOME | READ ON YOUR OWN

When you read passages in the Bible about Jesus being the *Bridegroom* and the church being the *bride*, images of modern-day engagements and weddings likely come to mind. Today, it is tradition for the man to ask the father (or family) of his prospective bride for her hand in marriage. He then proposes to her, often by getting down on one knee and presenting her with a ring. If she says yes, the couple is engaged, and they start planning the wedding ceremony and reception. Friends and family are invited to celebrate this joyous day.

The problem with these images is that ancient Jewish weddings were quite different. Back in Jesus' day, the father chose the bride. The groom would then meet with the bride's parents and present a written contract that included a "bride price," which was money given to compensate the bride's parents for the loss of her contribution to the family. Once the parties agreed to the contract, the deal was sealed with a glass of wine, and then the groom would depart to prepare a room in his father's house. Only when his father gave his approval could the groom return to claim his bride—and this could happen at any time.

Jesus' listeners would have had this context in mind when He spoke of the Bridegroom returning for His bride. Given this, it is important for us to know this context as well. This is the goal of this session: to view what Jesus taught through the lens of an ancient Jewish wedding.

OPEN | 10 MINUTES

Get the session started by choosing one or both of the following questions to discuss together as a group:

- What is something that spoke to you in last week's personal study that you would like to share with the group?

  — *or* —

- What was the most memorable wedding that you attended? What in particular stood out that made it so memorable?

WATCH | 25 MINUTES

Now watch the video for this session. Below is an outline of the key points covered during the teaching. Record any key concepts that stand out to you.

OUTLINE

I. **The ancient Jewish wedding is a metaphor for God's plan of redemption.**
   A. In those days, the bride was typically chosen by the father of the groom.
   B. The father and son would then go to the family of the bride-to-be and present a *ketubah*—a written contract that outlined the terms of the wedding.
   C. Included in the contract was the *mohar*—the negotiated price the groom's family was willing to pay for the bride-to-be to join their family.
   D. A glass of wine was poured, and once the bride and groom drank that wine together, the couple would be deemed *betrothed*, which was a binding agreement.

II. **The betrothal period represents the believer's present walk of faith.**
   A. The groom would leave to prepare a wedding chamber at his father's house.
   B. The groom could return for his bride only when his father approved this room.
   C. The groom's return would come as a surprise. It often happened at night, with the attendants blowing horns (*shofroth*) and holding a torchlight procession.
   D. The groom would literally "snatch away" (*harpazo*) the bride and present to her the bridal chamber, the *huppah*, where the marriage would be consummated.

III. **The bride had responsibilities to perform while she waited.**
   A. The bride underwent a *mikvah*, a ceremonial immersion, to signify her new life.
   B. She created her wedding garment, packed, and secured a lamp with oil.
   C. The bride had to remain pure and in a state of readiness for the groom's return. This readiness reflected her devotion and preparation for the groom's arrival.

IV. **There are parallels between the ancient Jewish wedding and the church.**
   A. God chose the bride for His Son before the foundation of the world (Ephesians 1:4). He alone determines the day and hour of Jesus' return (Matthew 24:36).
   B. Jesus, the Groom, has gone to prepare a place for His bride in His Father's house. He will return when that place He is preparing for us is ready (John 14:2–3).
   C. Jesus paid the bride price with His own blood (1 Corinthians 6:20; Acts 20:28).
   D. The bride must abide in Him, staying pure for the ceremony (James 4:4).
   E. Our role is to invite others to the wedding feast, living as witnesses until our Groom returns.

NOTES

DISCUSS | 35 MINUTES

Discuss what you just watched by answering the following questions.

1. Weddings are meant to be joyful, but in the ancient Jewish wedding, every step carried prophetic meaning. What part of the symbolism stood out to you the most? Why?

2. Invite someone to read aloud John 14:2–3. Jesus used first-century Jewish "wedding language" in this passage to describe His return for His people. How does understanding the cultural context of a Jewish wedding deepen your anticipation for His coming?

3. The groom's delay in returning for his bride was part of the traditional Jewish wedding process. It revealed the bride's faithfulness and readiness for her groom. How does this help you understand why seasons of waiting matter in your spiritual life?

4. Ask someone to read aloud the parable of the ten virgins in Matthew 25:1–13. What stands out to you about the actions of the five wise virgins who were prepared from the groom's return? What might "keeping oil in your lamp" look like in your life today?

5. Reflect on the wedding feast of the Lamb that the apostle John describes in the book of Revelation. What gives you the most hope personally when you look forward to this event? What steps are you taking to invite others to attend this future wedding feast?

RESPOND | 10 MINUTES

The image of the ancient Jewish wedding reminds us that our relationship with Jesus is not one of distance but of devotion. The Groom has paid the bride price, sealed the covenant, and gone to prepare a place for us. Every prophecy and promise points toward the day when He will return for His bride. Until then, our role is to stay ready, faithful, hopeful, and full of love.

> Let us rejoice and be glad and give him glory! For the wedding of the Lamb has come, and his bride has made herself ready.
>
> **REVELATION 19:7**

What does it look like to "make yourself ready" in this season of life? How does knowing your Groom is preparing a place for you change the way that you move through ordinary days?

Underline the verbs in this passage: *rejoice*, *be glad*, *give*, and *made ready*. Which one speaks most directly to where your heart is right now? Why that term?

PRAY | 10 MINUTES

Thank God for inviting you into His story not just as an observer but as part of His church—the bride of Christ. Thank Him for His patience, for His promises, and for the home He is preparing for you. Ask Him to help you stay alert and grounded in your faith even when life feels unsteady and uncertain. Also pray to have a heart that lives ready for Jesus' return . . . not out of fear of His coming but out of love for Him.

SESSION THREE

PERSONAL STUDY

There is something about a wedding that stirs hope, joy, and excitement in us. The Bible invites us to experience these same feelings when it talks about Jesus' return. Scripture uses the picture of an ancient Jewish wedding to show that what's coming isn't the end of the world but the beginning of a celebration. Jesus isn't returning as a distant ruler but as a Groom who is returning for His bride. From His promise to "prepare a place" for us (John 14:2) to the "wedding of the Lamb" (Revelation 19:7), every prophecy that we find in the Bible is part of that great love story. The personal exercises for this week will help you dive deeper into these topics. As you work through them, write down your responses to the questions, as you will be given a few minutes to share your insights if you are doing this study with a group. If you are reading *The King Is Coming*, first review chapters 8–10 of the book.

You aren't in the dark
about these things,
dear brothers and sisters,
and you won't be surprised
when the day of the
Lord comes like a thief.

1 THESSALONIANS 5:4 NLT

STUDY 1

BUILT ON TRUST

If you've ever been part of a friendship, marriage, or team that truly works well together, you know the quiet power of trust. It's what allows people to relax, share responsibility, and dream together. Without it, even the strongest love or best intention starts to unravel. This is why trust sits at the heart of God's plan for His people. Yet love and trust are not the same. God's love is unconditional, but His trust must be proven. Just as a marriage grows stronger through shared trials, so our faith matures through testing.

This isn't punishment; it's preparation. Every act of obedience in the unseen places of life is shaping our eternal role in the unseen kingdom.

Jesus modeled this first. He loved people, but He "would not entrust himself" to the crowds (John 2:24) because He knew human hearts. Over time, though, He found a few who stayed—disciples who stuck through confusion, persecution, and failure. By the end of His ministry, He called them His "friends" (15:15). They had become trustworthy. This is the picture of what God is forming in you. The more you stay faithful under pressure, the deeper your bond with Christ grows. In eternity, that trust becomes the foundation of shared authority.

The idea of reigning with Christ might feel distant or abstract. But think about it this way. This life is your *internship* for eternity. How you lead, forgive, serve, and persevere in the present is shaping what He can entrust to you in the future. So, if life feels hard or repetitive right now, remember that your loyalty is not going unnoticed. You are becoming the kind of person whom Jesus can confide in, collaborate with, and celebrate with for eternity. He is not just saving you for heaven but is also shaping you to share His heart here on earth.

1. James wrote, "Consider it pure joy, my brothers and sisters, whenever you face trials of many kinds, because you know that the testing of your faith produces perseverance" (1:2–3). Which areas of your life right now feel like they're testing your trust in God's timing or character? How might those moments actually be strengthening your faith in Him?

2. Read Jesus' words to His disciples in John 15:12–17. In the table below, write down what commands Jesus gives and how He describes those who are His *friends*.

Passage	Command / How Jesus describes who are His friends
verse 12	
verse 14	
verse 15	
verse 17	

> There are believers who are concerned they're not going to like the eternal state as much as this present life. Many imagine us being transformed into some sort of ethereal beings, living in a world without substance and void of anything exciting to do. They imagine we will all be part of a nonstop church or worship service. Oh, how far from the truth! All that's seen has been created by what cannot be seen. . . . It's ludicrous to imagine our world coming forth from a boring or inferior one in recreation, adventure, creativity, development, expansion, innovation, the arts, or any other exciting aspect of this life. It's laughable when you say it out loud, yet some wrestle with these very deep-seated concerns. The eternal will consist of all the godly pleasures, joys, excitement, and beauty of this life but will be considerably better and perfect in every regard.[16]

3. Read 1 Corinthians 2:9–10. When you think about eternity, do you imagine something distant and dull . . . or alive and full of purpose? How does this verse reshape your picture of the life to come and the way you live for Christ now?

4. David declared, "I remain confident of this: I will see the goodness of the Lord in the land of the living. Wait for the Lord; be strong and take heart and wait for the Lord" (Psalm 27:13–14). How did David express his trust in God? How do you think this allowed him to "be strong" and "take heart" as he waited for the Lord to move on his behalf?

In God's wisdom, He determined those who'd forever govern with Him would be those who proved their loyalty in hostile enemy territory. These coleaders refused to submit to pressures created by the rebellious forces, choosing to suffer and endure hardships in their obedience. Their trustworthiness would be forever sealed by enduring to the end. For this reason, Paul writes: "If we endure hardship, we will reign with Him" (2 Timothy 2:12 NLT). Jesus chose to initiate the path; He, as Pioneer, faced the most severe testing. We read, "He humbled himself in obedience to God and died a criminal's death on a cross. Therefore, God elevated him to the place of highest honor" (Philippians 2:8–9 NLT). His loyalty was forever proven, so God declared to His faithful Son: "Your throne, O God, endures forever and ever" (Hebrews 1:8 NLT).[17]

5. Reflect on Paul's statement that "if we endure hardship, we will reign with Him" (2 Timothy 2:12 NLT). When you think of the hardship you've endured for the sake of Christ, how has that grown your trust in Him?

How might this hardship be preparing you to *reign* with Him?

STUDY 2

RIGHT ON TIME

God's promises never run late. They unfold exactly at the time He intends—often in ways that remind us that He's been several steps ahead all along. The timeline of prophecy isn't *random* but *precise*. Centuries before Jesus' first coming, prophets recorded the year and even the week of His death. When the appointed time came, every word was fulfilled exactly as spoken.

The same precision still holds today. The same God who fulfilled His Word at the cross continues to move history toward another moment of fulfillment: the return of Jesus. While we don't know the exact "day or hour" (Mark 13:32), we are told to recognize the season. Every fulfilled prophecy—whether it is Israel's rebirth in 1948 or the city of Jerusalem being returned to Israel from Gentile control in 1967—reveals that God's timeline is alive and active.

Understanding prophecy isn't about decoding headlines or predicting dates but about remembering who is writing the story. When we see His promises keeping pace with history, we are reminded that nothing is slipping out of His control . . . not the world, not our lives, and especially not our waiting. For a generation that measures time by calendars and notifications, prophecy teaches us to rest in *divine* timing. As we have seen, Jesus compared His return to the rhythm of a wedding. He let us know it is all about the Groom coming back when the Father says it is time. This means waiting isn't wasted; it's just part of the preparation.

If you're feeling like God's promises have been delayed or forgotten, look again at the timeline that He has already kept. The same faithfulness that guided every step of Israel's story is guiding yours. His clock hasn't stopped ticking . . . and He has never missed an appointment.

1. Read Habakkuk 2:3. Where do you feel like you're waiting for something that God has promised? How does remembering that His timing is *perfect* change your posture as you wait?

2. In order to fully grasp the message of Jesus (the Groom) returning "right on time" for His bride (the church), it is helpful to view what the Bible teaches through the lens of a first-century Jewish wedding. Look up the following passages and write down what the accompanying wedding imagery reveals about the return of Jesus to this world.

The bride was chosen by the father of the groom.
Ephesians 1:4: ______

The father and son would present a contract that outlined the terms of the wedding. Included in the contract was the "bride price."
1 Corinthians 6:20: ______

The groom would leave to prepare a wedding chamber at his father's house.
John 14:2–3: ______

The bride underwent a ceremonial immersion to signify her new life.
Ephesians 5:25–27: ______

The groom could return for his bride only upon his father's consent.
Matthew 24:36: ______

The groom's return for his bride would come as a surprise.
Matthew 25:5–6: ______________________________

The groom would "snatch away" the bride to take her to his father's home.
1 Thessalonians 4:17–18: ______________________________

The disciples were admiring the temple complex, commenting on the stunning beauty of the buildings. Jesus seized the moment to inform them of the approaching devastating destruction and went so far as to say that not one stone would be left upon another. He was foretelling Titus and Rome coming forty years later and utterly destroying the temple and Jerusalem. His disciples then asked, "Tell us, when will all this happen?" (Matthew 24:3 NLT). . . . Look at Jesus' concluding words concerning the devastation of AD 70: "They will be killed by the sword or sent away as captives to all the nations of the world. And Jerusalem will be trampled down by the Gentiles until the period of the Gentiles comes to an end" (Luke 21:24 NLT).[18]

---

3. Jesus' prophecy in Luke 21:24 has already come to life through history and continues to echo in our present day. How does knowing that His words about Jerusalem came true affect your confidence in the prophecies that have yet to be fulfilled? What does this teach you about how God keeps His word both globally and personally?

4. Now read Luke 21:28. What might it look like to lift up your head in daily life . . . to live alert and hopeful rather than distracted or anxious as the world changes?

Jesus speaks of the signs—birth pangs (see Matthew 24:8). Just as a woman's birth contractions become increasingly more frequent and intense, even so the signs in the sun, moon, stars, earthquakes, tsunamis, plagues, pestilence, famines, and others Jesus speaks of have done the same. They will become even more frequent and intense as we approach His return. Then we come to the climax: *His coming in great glory*, and *every eye* will see Him. I love the words of the apostle John: "Behold, He is coming with clouds, and *every eye will see Him*, even they who pierced Him. And all the tribes of the earth will mourn because of Him. Even so, Amen" (Revelation 1:7 NKJV).[19]

---

5. Review Matthew 24:4–8. Jesus describes the signs of His return in this passage as birth pains growing closer together and more intense with time. What does Jesus say is His purpose in giving the warning about false messiahs? Why do His followers not need to be alarmed when they hear about "wars and rumors of wars" (verse 6)?

STUDY 3

READY OR NOT

The Bible doesn't whisper about the return of Jesus. It shouts it from Genesis to Revelation! John writes that "every eye will see him" (Revelation 1:7). The day when love and justice meet face-to-face will be both glorious and sobering. Some will be ready. Many will not.

Remember that Jesus described the signs of His coming as birth pains—intense, unmistakable, and increasingly close together. Earthquakes, wars, plagues, and upheaval aren't random headlines but reminders that history is moving toward fulfillment of this prophecy. For believers in Christ, prophecy reminds us of the beginning of reunion, restoration, and reward.

God's justice is as real as His mercy. But His judgment is not cruelty. Just as a loving parent sets boundaries to guard what is precious, so God will one day purify His creation from everything that destroys. He will not let evil last forever. This reality calls for *readiness*. As John reveals, a time is coming when the righteous will remain righteous and the wicked will remain wicked (see Revelation 22:11). The choices we make now echo into all time. The question is not when Jesus will return but whether we are living as if He could come today.

For believers in Christ, this truth should anchor us. We don't have to predict dates or live in panic. We live in purpose. We pursue holiness not to earn Jesus' love but to reflect it. When the King returns, He won't be searching for perfection. He'll be looking for hearts that stayed loyal, lamps that stayed lit, and faith that stayed alive. The story of redemption will close where it began: in God's presence, with His people walking together in peace.

1. Many people try to prepare for the future in practical ways such as by stocking up, planning ahead, or even prepping for the unknown. What is the equivalent of this kind of *spiritual* preparation when it comes to being ready and watching for Jesus' return?

2. Read 2 Peter 3:10–12. Peter asks, "Since everything will be destroyed in this way"—referring to what will occur in the Day of the Lord—"what kind of people ought you to be?" (verse 11). How does Peter answer this question? How might this reminder reshape how you spend your time, pursue your goals, or make decisions in this current season?

John the apostle wrote, "I saw an angel standing in the sun, shouting to the vultures flying high in the sky: 'Come! Gather together for the great banquet God has prepared. Come and eat the flesh of kings, generals, and strong warriors; of horses and their riders; and of all humanity, both free and slave, small and great'" (Revelation 19:17–18 NLT). Scripture declares that on that day, humanity will be "scarcer than gold" (Isaiah 13:12 NLT). . . . Think of all the terrible natural disasters, hellish wars, horrendous genocides, devastating plagues, and other past horrific sufferings of the human race. None of them will compare to what is coming.[20]

---

3. John the apostle, in Revelation 19:17–18, paints a picture of God's justice being fully seen on earth. How does knowing that God's *ultimate* justice will one day be carried out shape the way you respond to injustice, cruelty, or suffering in the world right now? (You might want to reflect on Paul's words in Romans 12:19–21 before answering.)

4. For centuries, godly men and women have been crying out to warn people of the coming wrath of God. Cyprian of Carthage, writing around AD 251, stated the following:

> And therefore the Lord, looking to our days, says in His Gospel, "When the Son of man comes, think you that He shall find faith on the earth?" [Luke 18:8]. We see that what He foretold has come to pass. There is no faith in the fear of God, in the law of righteousness, in love, in labor; none considers the fear of futurity, and none takes to heart the day of the Lord, and the wrath of God, and the punishments to come upon unbelievers, and the eternal torments decreed for the faithless.[21]

Cyprian was a godly voice crying out some 1,800 years ago, but his warnings are just as relevant today. Why is it critical for believers to *keep* following Jesus' command to "go into all the world and preach the gospel to all creation" (Mark 16:15)? What is the result when believers in Christ get complacent about warning people of God's coming wrath?

How can God put all that is pure and lovely in harm's way? How could He allow this? If He did, He would be cruel, not loving. Because He truly is love, therefore He protects.

When Adam chose the nature of sin and death, God quickly drove the first couple out of the garden to protect them. If they would have partaken of the Tree of Life, they would have been doomed to keep their evil nature forever, thus making mankind forever an adversary to God's nature of righteousness and goodness. Mankind would have been eternally evil, as Satan and His hordes are. Love rescued those who would choose to worship Him.

God has been patient; He has been longsuffering; He wants everyone to repent and come to eternal life through the lordship of Jesus Christ. But as time passes, mankind's heart grows harder and harder, and there is coming a time—and it's so soon—when, if those who remain were given a thousand more years, they wouldn't change. . . . In the day of His coming there will be no in-between. We read: "Everyone will see the LORD's hand of blessing on his servants—and his anger against his enemies" (Isaiah 66:14 NLT).[22]

5. David wrote, "As a father has compassion on his children, so the LORD has compassion on those who fear him" (Psalm 103:13). A loving parent doesn't let a child play with fire or run into traffic. How has God's discipline in your life proven to be an act of His compassion? From what has God saved you as a result of His loving discipline and correction?

CATCH UP AND CONNECT

Consider connecting with a fellow group member sometime this week to discuss some of your key insights from this session. Use any of the following prompts to help guide your discussion.

- How does the imagery of the *ketubah* (written marriage contract) and *mohar* (bride price) help you understand what God did when He redeemed you?
- In what ways does a believer's present walk of faith with Christ mirror the betrothal period of an ancient Jewish wedding?
- What was the bride's responsibility in an ancient Jewish wedding as she waited for her groom to return? What is a believer in Christ's responsibility when it comes to waiting for Jesus—the Bridegroom—to appear?
- What do you do to stay spiritually awake and ready for Jesus' return? What preparations are you making now in anticipation of His return?
- As you think about what is ahead, what part of God's future plan excites or motivates you the most to live with greater purpose today?

Use this time to go back and complete any of the study and reflection questions from previous days that you weren't able to finish. Make a note below of any revelations you've had and reflect on any growth or personal insights you've gained.

NEXT WEEK'S READING: **Chapters 11–13 in *The King Is Coming***

WEEK 4 *at a glance*

THIS WEEK'S READING	**Chapters 11–13 in *The King Is Coming***
GROUP MEETING	Read the Welcome and Open the group (page 68) Watch the video and take notes (pages 69–70) Discuss the questions that follow (page 71) Respond to the teaching and Pray (page 72)
PERSONAL STUDIES: **STUDY 1** **STUDY 2** **STUDY 3**	 **"Look Up" (pages 75–78)** **"Check Your Source" (pages 79–82)** **"No Snooze Button" (pages 83–86)**
CATCH UP AND CONNECT	Connect with someone in your group Complete any unfinished studies (page 87)
NEXT WEEK'S READING (BEFORE WEEK 5 GROUP MEETING)	**Chapters 14–21 in *The King Is Coming***

SESSION FOUR

IS IT THE SEASON OF JESUS' RETURN?

"Be on guard! Be alert! You do not know when that time will come."

MARK 13:33

WELCOME | READ ON YOUR OWN

Earthquakes. Wars. Political tension. Cultural chaos. Open any news app and it seems the world is shaking from every direction. But none of this takes God by surprise. He has revealed in His Word that calamity and chaos *will* increase as we approach the end times.

Jesus, in one notable teaching to His disciples, even described certain signs that would increase in intensity, like birth pains, to signal the coming of the end (see Mark 13:1–31). However, He ended that teaching by saying, "But about that day or hour no one knows, not even the angels in heaven, nor the Son, but only the Father. Be on guard! Be alert! You do not know when that time will come" (verses 32–33). Jesus wanted His followers to be aware of the end times not so they would be *alarmed* but so they would remain *alert*. The warnings He gave served as instructions for them to stay in a state of readiness for His return.

In this session, you will explore how biblical prophecy gives you a way to read the times without losing your peace. You will see that while the headlines may shift daily, God's storyline always remains the same. He is the one who "connects the dots," and He invites you to look at the events that are happening around you through the lens of His eyes rather than the world's turmoil. In this way, you can follow Jesus' command to stay vigilant—watching and waiting for His return—as you go about the tasks that He has given you to do on this earth.

OPEN | 10 MINUTES

Get the session started by choosing one or both of the following questions to discuss together as a group:

- What is something that spoke to you in last week's personal study that you would like to share with the group?

  — *or* —

- When you look at what is happening in the world today (news headlines, global conflicts, natural disasters), how do you tend to respond?

WATCH | 25 MINUTES

Now watch the video for this session. Below is an outline of the key points covered during the teaching. Record any key concepts that stand out to you.

OUTLINE

I. **Believers in Christ are called to seek out the "mysteries" of God.**
   A. As one author wrote, "It is the glory of God to conceal a matter; to search out a matter is the glory of kings" (Proverbs 25:2).
   B. As "kings and priests," we are called to examine Scripture carefully, like the Bereans were commended for doing (Acts 17:11), to confirm God's truth.
   C. Believers walking in the Spirit sense internally that it is the season of Jesus' return.

II. **Believers in Jesus *cannot* know for certain the exact time of His return.**
   A. Jesus Himself said that no one can know the exact day or hour of His return. God the Father alone determines the timing (Mark 13:32).
   B. However, while the exact *time* is unknown, Jesus (and the apostles) expect believers to recognize the *time frame* (1 Thessalonians 5:4).
   C. Understanding the signs of the times is essential. God's concealment is meant not to confuse us but to invite pursuit and discernment.

III. **Israel's rebirth as a nation marks the prophetic shift into the final time frame.**
   A. Jesus' prophecy about the destruction of the temple was fulfilled in AD 70 when the Roman general Titus leveled the city of Jerusalem.
   B. Israel's rebirth on May 14, 1948, fulfilled Isaiah's prophecy of "a country . . . born in a day" and "a nation . . . brought forth in a moment" (66:8).
   C. "Jerusalem will be trampled on by the Gentiles until the times of the Gentiles are fulfilled" (Luke 21:24). This was fulfilled in 1967 when Israel regained Jerusalem.
   D. These prophecies, once considered inexplicable, are now fulfilled, which confirms that this generation is living in the prophetic window that Jesus described.

IV. **Every fulfilled prophecy points to the nearness of Jesus' return.**
   A. From the rebirth of Israel to the regathering of nations, no major prophecy in the Bible remains unfulfilled.
   B. God's "delay" in sending Jesus back is an act of His mercy, for He does not want "anyone to perish, but everyone to come to repentance" (2 Peter 3:9).
   C. We should live with a dual focus: planning responsibly for the future while walking in readiness today. We plan as if Jesus' return is far off but live as if it is imminent.

NOTES

DISCUSS | 35 MINUTES

Discuss what you just watched by answering the following questions.

1. Jesus told His followers that "only the Father" knows the *day* of His return (Matthew 24:36). However, He gave them clues to help them know the *time frame* of His return. What are some of the "signs of the season" mentioned in this session that stand out to you?

2. Read Isaiah 66:8. The prophet described a country being "born in a day." How does the modern rebirth of Israel in 1948 help confirm God's faithfulness to prophecy? What does this event stir in your faith about God's timing?

3. Jesus foretold of Jerusalem being "trampled on by the Gentiles until the times of the Gentiles are fulfilled" (Luke 21:24). The "times of the Gentiles" came to an end when the city of Jerusalem returned to Jewish rule in 1967. How could recognizing this shift in the prophetic landscape shape the way you pray, live, and view global events today?

4. Ask someone to read 2 Peter 3:8–9. What does a "day" represent to the Lord? What does this passage reveal about God's long-term plan for redemption?

5. Believers should *plan like Jesus is not coming back for two hundred years but live as if He is returning today*. How could that mindset help you stay spiritually awake and "on fire" while remaining grounded in your everyday responsibilities?

RESPOND | 10 MINUTES

God's Word reminds us that the same Lord who fulfilled His promises in the past will fulfill the ones still ahead. The timeline of history is being *directed* by a faithful God. Take a few moments to read the passage below and reflect on how it connects to what you have learned in this session.

> "Learn this lesson from the fig tree: As soon as its twigs get tender and its leaves come out, you know that summer is near. Even so, when you see all these things, you know that it is near, right at the door. Truly I tell you, this generation will certainly not pass away until all these things have happened."
>
> **MATTHEW 24:32-34**

What is the "lesson from the fig tree" that Jesus teaches His disciples?

What does this lesson say about the importance of recognizing the prophetic time frame that believers are in?

PRAY | 10 MINUTES

As you close this session, thank God for the assurance that His timeline is perfect. Praise Him for being a God who reveals truth through prophecy and who remains faithful through every generation. Ask Him to steady your heart when the world feels uncertain and remind you that He is not distant or delayed but right on schedule. Invite the Holy Spirit to fill you with peace that steadies your emotions and courage that strengthens your witness for Christ.

SESSION FOUR

PERSONAL STUDY

Every generation has faced world events that shake their sense of control. Wars, natural disasters, pandemics, and global instability remind us that history is not random but is unfolding toward a divine purpose. The content you will explore in the personal studies this week will reveal just how intentional that plan is. From the prophetic patterns of Israel's story to the warnings Jesus gave His disciples, God's timeline has always been right on schedule—even when humanity has misunderstood the clock. Jesus doesn't call us to predict dates, but He does call us to stay close. Just as the early church learned to live with both urgency and peace, so can we. As you work through these exercises, continue to write down your responses, as you will be given a few minutes to share your insights if you are doing this study with a group. If you are reading *The King Is Coming*, first review chapters 11–13 of the book.

"I tell you the truth, this generation will not pass from the scene before all these things take place."

MARK 13:30 NLT

STUDY 1

LOOK UP

Jesus told His followers that when they saw certain signs beginning to unfold, they were to "stand up" and "lift up" their heads, because their redemption was near (Luke 21:28). These words were meant to awaken our hearts. Just as contractions signal the nearness of birth, so the unrest and shaking of the world remind us that God's plan is still on track.

When life feels uncertain, the easiest posture is to hunch over and become absorbed by work, schedules, and newsfeeds. But Jesus calls us to do the opposite. The Greek word for *stand up* in Luke 21:28 carries the idea of straightening up after being bent over. It's the act of refusing to live slouched under distraction or discouragement. To *look up* means to be aware of heaven's reality—setting our focus not on temporary noise but on eternal truth.

Paul echoed these ideas in Colossians 3:1–2: "Set your hearts on things above, where Christ is, seated at the right hand of God. Set your minds on things above, not on earthly things." *Setting our minds* means choosing our perspective. It doesn't mean ignoring real problems but seeing them through the lens of God's sovereign plan. The world's instability isn't the end of the story but a reminder we are getting closer to the restoration God promised.

So when the weight of the world pulls your gaze downward, pause, stand, and look up. You are meant to live alert and alive in hope. This isn't about predicting dates or deciphering headlines. It's about choosing to live in awareness and readiness—knowing that every sunrise moves you one day closer to being in the presence of your Redeemer.

1. Paul's instruction in Colossians 3:2 is to "set your minds on things above." If your sights are set on things of this life, and you only *periodically* glance at the realities of heaven, you can easily be lulled to sleep. What are three things that tempt you to *set* your mind on them at the expense of setting your mind on heaven? List those in the space below.

-
-
-

2. Read Psalm 121:1–8. What does it mean for you to "lift up [your] eyes" (verse 1) toward God when life feels uncertain or the world seems unstable? What promises does this passage provide for those who choose to set their sights on God in this way?

Picture a betrothed bride in ancient Jewish times. Her groom has been away for almost a year, and she's expectant and prepared for that special evening when the shouts and blowing shofars will ring throughout her community's streets. Her lamp is bedside, her trunk is packed, and her wedding garment and veil hang in a prominent spot in her bedroom. Though his return was imminent from their first day away from each other, she's keenly aware it's now the most probable time frame for him to catch her away.[23]

3. Think about this imagery of a bride waiting for her groom. She understands that it is the season of his return. In what ways is every believer in a similar place? What can we know about the time frame we are in?

4. Paul wrote that "our citizenship is in heaven" and that "we eagerly await a Savior from there" (Philippians 3:20). What does it mean that your citizenship is in heaven? How should this impact how you view today's news, your priorities, or your sense of purpose?

Consider the bride-in-waiting, who has her daily tasks at her parents' home: prepare food, do laundry, get water from the well, or various other chores; however, in this season her sights are *set* on her soon coming groom. Her thoughts go to his coming whenever they are not required for the daily tasks.

Where do you find your thoughts going when your mind is in neutral? This is where they are *set.* If you incessantly think about and are consumed by the stats of your favorite NCAA team, increasing your followers on YouTube or Instagram, making money, and . . . the list is almost endless . . . you're slouched over. Your mind is *set* on a world that is quickly passing away. If you belong to Jesus, you died to this world and your life is hidden with Christ in God.[24]

5. Paul, after instructing believers to set their minds "on things above," made this interesting comment: "For you died, and your life is now hidden with Christ in God" (Colossians 3:2–3). Would you say your daily mindset is that you have *died* to this world? If not, what would change in your priorities if you truly viewed your time on earth in this way?

STUDY 2

CHECK YOUR SOURCE

You've probably experienced that moment when something you thought was true turned out to *not* be true. Maybe the photo was AI generated, or the "breaking news" came from an unreliable post, or other embellishments were made. In an age when misinformation spreads faster than truth, the lesson is to *always check your source.*

Peter's warning that "in the last days scoffers will come" (2 Peter 3:3) feels relevant today. In his time, false teachers and skeptics were mocking the promise of Christ's return. They claimed that because time kept moving and the world looked the same, God's Word must be wrong. Peter called out that thinking for what it was: *forgetfulness*. They had forgotten the same God who spoke creation into being also judged it in Noah's day. They had forgotten the Lord is not slow but patient, giving people space to repent before the final day arrives.

The ancient Jewish rabbis taught of a seven-day world history pattern, with each "day" symbolizing a thousand years. Similarly, humanity's story would unfold over six days—six thousand years of labor, struggle, and redemption—culminating in a seventh-day rest that mirrored God's Sabbath. It was outlined like this: the Age of Creation (2,000 years), the Age of the Law (2,000 years), the Age of Grace (2,000 years), and the Kingdom Age (1,000 years).

It's likely we are standing at the close of the sixth day, roughly two thousand years after the cross. That's not a date-setting formula but a reminder that history is moving toward fulfillment exactly as God planned. The news cycle changes hourly, yet God's story never has. In a world that constantly updates, prophecy invites us to lock ourselves in to what doesn't.

1. Peter writes, "The day of the Lord will come like a thief. The heavens will disappear with a roar; the elements will be destroyed by fire, and the earth and everything done in it will be laid bare" (2 Peter 3:10). Imagine you knew an unexpected guest was arriving—not to steal but to inspect everything you've built. What would you want them to find in your life?

2. The Bible reveals that God often moves in ways that surprise people. These are moments that arrive "like a thief," catching even the faithful off guard. Look up the following passages in which God's actions came suddenly or unexpectedly, and then write down what they reveal about God's timing, mercy, and justice.

Passage	What this reveals about God's timing, mercy, and justice
Genesis 6:11–7:10	
Exodus 12:1–30	
Luke 2:1–21	
Acts 9:1–19	

"I will be like a lion to Israel, like a strong young lion to Judah. I will tear them to pieces! I will carry them off, and no one will be left to rescue them. Then I will *return to my place* until they admit their guilt and turn to me. For as soon as trouble comes, they will earnestly search for me" (Hosea 5:14-15 NLT, emphasis added). Hosea is speaking to the Jewish nation, but in doing so, we get a glimpse of the church's time period.

There are two major times that God permitted Israel and Judah to be torn into pieces. The first was the Babylonian invasion. If you search the Scriptures, you'll find out the Chaldeans were ruthless with the Jewish people, including women, children, and babies. A small remnant survived and were taken to Babylon, but most were brutally slaughtered. The other occasion was Titus's conquest of the city of Jerusalem in AD 70, culminating in Rome's utter depopulation of Israel over the next few decades.

The question is, which incident is God addressing through the prophet Hosea? The simple answer: It's definitely the Roman devastation spanning from AD 70 to 132.[25]

3. God, speaking through Hosea, says that He will withdraw from His people "until they admit their guilt and turn to me" (5:15 NLT). God here is *temporarily* stepping back to allow His people to face the consequences of their sin. How does this prophecy point to both judgment and restoration? How does this idea of God "returning to His place" help you to see why He is allowing certain things to take place in the world today?

There is a key statement in Hosea 5:15: "I will return to my place" (NLT). To "return" means you have to leave a specific location, go somewhere, and then go back to the specific location you started from. Jesus left "His place" with the Father approximately two thousand years ago and *returned* to

His place thirty-three years later. Shortly afterward Israel was "torn into pieces" by Rome.

Continuing on: "Come, and let us return to the LORD; for He has torn, but He will heal us; He has stricken, but He will bind us up. *After two days* He will revive us; on the third day He will raise us up, that we may live in His sight" (Hosea 6:1–2 NKJV, emphasis added). Israel as a nation eventually cries out, "Come let us return to the Lord." When will this happen? After two days! Remember what Peter said: A day with the Lord is as one thousand years. Hosea is saying "after two thousand years." We have the timing!

What happens during these two thousand years? In a general sense, the Jewish people are blinded to the redemption available to mankind. God focuses on the Gentiles during this period. This is the Age of Grace—the church age, in which the Gentiles (and most definitely some Jewish people) come to salvation.[26]

4. Hosea 6:1–2 reveals that we are currently living in the Age of Grace—the church age—in which God's focus is on the Gentiles. What does Paul say about this age in Romans 11:25–26? What does Peter add about this time in Acts 15:13–15?

5. Read Hosea 6:3. When you "check the source" (God's Word) it becomes clear we are living in the *time frame* of Jesus' return. How does Hosea advise you to live in light of this truth? What does He say about the certainty of Jesus' appearance?

STUDY 3

NO SNOOZE BUTTON

If you've ever stayed up late tracking a storm alert on your phone, you know what it's like to stay *watchful*. You glance at updates, refresh the page, and check your notifications because you don't want to miss what's coming. Spiritually speaking, Jesus used the same image when He told His followers to "watch and pray" (Matthew 26:41). He wasn't asking for paranoia or fear but for presence. To "watch" is to live aware of what God is doing now and what He has promised to do next. It is to keep us from pressing the spiritual snooze button.

The early believers lived with this kind of focus. They didn't know when Jesus would return but they believed it could be any day. This expectancy shaped how they loved people, prayed, and endured hardship. Two thousand years later, we sometimes confuse delay for distance. Yet God's timing hasn't changed—only our attention has. Like the servant in Jesus' parable who grew careless because his master seemed delayed (see Luke 12:35–48), we risk drifting into apathy when we forget that waiting is part of preparation.

Watching doesn't mean staring at the sky. It means tending to our prayer life, keeping our conscience clear, and staying sensitive to the Holy Spirit's nudges in the middle of everyday life. It means choosing to notice God in the noise. Jesus instructed us to "watch and pray." The pairing is important. We can't stay watchful without staying connected.

In a culture constantly refreshing its feeds, perhaps the most radical thing we can do is pause, turn off the noise, and turn our attention toward heaven, remembering that watching isn't about *predicting* but about being *present* to the One who is already near.

1. Read Habakkuk 2:1. The "watchtower" (NLT) was a place of both observation and protection in ancient times. If you pictured your life as a watchtower, what distractions, influences, or habits might you need to clear away in order to clearly see what God is doing?

2. Read 1 Thessalonians 5:6–8. What analogy does Paul use to describe how believers in Christ are to discern what God is doing *now* and what He has promised to do in the *future*? How does Paul say you should live given that you "belong to the day"?

"Take heed, *watch* and pray; for you do not know when the time is. . . . *Watch* therefore, for you do not know when the master of the house is coming—in the evening, at midnight, at the crowing of the rooster, or in the morning. . . . And what I say to you, I say to all: *Watch!*" (Mark 13:33, 35, 37 NKJV, emphasis added).

There are a few things to highlight in Mark's account. First, in just four verses Jesus commands us to "watch" three separate times! This alone should get our attention in a huge way. Second, He adds the word "pray" in verse 33. We keep watch by staying in prayer. Paul instructed the Thessalonian church, immediately after writing of the Lord's imminent return, to "never stop praying" (1 Thessalonians 5:17 NLT).

How can we do this? If prayer is limited to going into a closet, shutting the door, and making requests, then this command is impossible. We must remember, prayer is not a monologue, rather, it is a dialogue. It's communion with God. Sometimes there are words, but not always.[27]

---

3. Jesus used the word *watch* three times in just four verses—a repetition that suggests urgency and focus. Paul echoed the same truth when he wrote, "Never stop praying" (1 Thessalonians 5:17 NLT). How does cultivating prayer as an *ongoing conversation*—rather than just a *task*—help you stay spiritually awake in today's distracted world?

4. Which "signal strength" best describes your prayer connection right now? Place a check mark next to the one that describes you.

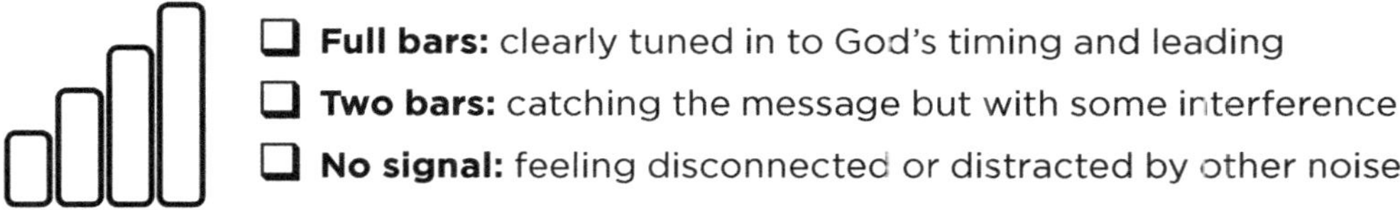

- ❑ **Full bars:** clearly tuned in to God's timing and leading
- ❑ **Two bars:** catching the message but with some interference
- ❑ **No signal:** feeling disconnected or distracted by other noise

What would most help you to strengthen your signal this week?

We are instructed to not only watch but to be sober, especially refraining from slipping into a state of sleep. The word *sober* is defined as "to be in control of one's thought processes and thus not be in danger of irrational thinking."[28] When Jesus warned, "People will be terrified at what they see coming upon the earth" (Luke 21:26 NLT), the importance of staying in control of our thought processes is made clear.[29]

5. Think about all that you've covered this week as it relates to the timing and season of Jesus' return. Which image below best describes your current confidence in the prophecy you've covered? (Reflect on how this has changed from when you first started this Bible study.)

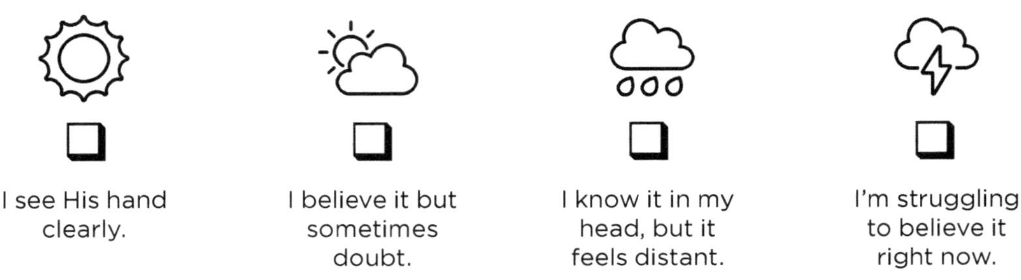

Why did you respond in this way? What questions are still lingering in your mind regarding the time frame of Christ's return?

CATCH UP AND CONNECT

Consider connecting with a fellow group member sometime this week to discuss your key insights from this session. Use any of the following prompts to help guide your discussion.

- What insight from this week's study challenged how you think about staying spiritually awake in today's world? Why do you think it stood out?
- What did you learn this week about what it means to set your mind on things above? How easy is it for you to keep your focus on heavenly things?
- In an age filled with fears and distractions, how can you remain alert without being anxious? What role does prayer play in that balance?
- Prayer isn't only about asking but also listening. How can you make more room in your week for that kind of communion with God?
- As you look ahead to the next session, what question do you have about prophecy, prayer, or the future that you hope will become clearer?

Use this time to go back and complete any of the study and reflection questions from previous days that you weren't able to finish. Make a note below of any revelations you've had and reflect on any growth or personal insights you've gained.

NEXT WEEK'S READING: Chapters 14–21 in *The King Is Coming*

WEEK 5 *at a glance*

THIS WEEK'S READING	Chapters 14–21 in *The King Is Coming*
GROUP MEETING	Read the Welcome and Open the group (page 90) Watch the video and take notes (pages 91–92) Discuss the questions that follow (page 93) Respond to the teaching and Pray (page 94)
PERSONAL STUDIES:	
STUDY 1	"Both Groom and King" (pages 97–100)
STUDY 2	"Holding the Line" (pages 101–104)
STUDY 3	"Pure and Ready" (pages 105–108)
CATCH UP AND CONNECT	Connect with someone in your group Complete any unfinished studies (page 109)
NEXT WEEK'S READING (BEFORE WEEK 6 GROUP MEETING)	Chapters 22–28 in *The King Is Coming*

SESSION FIVE

THE CATCHING AWAY OF HIS BRIDE

You are all children of the light and children of the day. We do not belong to the night or to the darkness. So then, let us not be like others, who are asleep, but let us be awake and sober.

1 THESSALONIANS 5:5–6

WELCOME | READ ON YOUR OWN

In ancient Jewish weddings, the father would commission his son to "snatch away" his bride when the dwelling was ready. In the same way, God the Father will commission His Son, Jesus, to return to earth to snatch away His bride, the church. All of Scripture—from Genesis to Revelation—points to this climactic moment. The same Jesus who entered Jerusalem on a donkey will return on a white horse, crowned with many crowns, and every eye will see Him.

The wedding invitation, promising the joy of being joined to Christ, has gone out to all. Those who accept the offer are immediately transformed "from death to life" (John 5:24) and then, as they cooperate with the work of the Holy Spirit, are transformed "by the renewing of [their] mind" (Romans 12:2). But there is a final transformation! As Paul writes, "We will all be changed—in a flash, in the twinkling of an eye, at the last trumpet. For the trumpet will sound, the dead will be raised imperishable, and we will be changed" (1 Corinthians 15:51–52).

In this session, you will explore what will take place when the bride (the church) is "caught up" (1 Thessalonians 4:17) to be joined with the Bridegroom (Christ) at the last trumpet. Jesus *will* return in glory to establish His kingdom on earth. "He will appear a second time, not to bear sin, but to bring salvation to those who are waiting for him" (Hebrews 9:28).

OPEN | 10 MINUTES

Get the session started by choosing one or both of the following questions to discuss together as a group:

- What is something that spoke to you in last week's personal study that you would like to share with the group?

  — *or* —

- If you could go back to any moment in history and watch God at work (like a behind-the-scenes view), what scene would you choose? Why?

WATCH | 25 MINUTES

Now watch the video for this session. Below is an outline of the key points covered during the teaching. Record any key concepts that stand out to you.

OUTLINE

I. **Believers are to be ready for Jesus' return but also work until He returns.**
   A. Jesus commands believers, "Occupy till I come" (Luke 19:13 KJV), which indicates the need for us to balance long-term planning with daily readiness for His return.
   B. Slacking off or neglecting our responsibilities contradicts Jesus' directive to remain diligent and faithful in our endeavors until He returns.
   C. This mindset fosters holiness, urgency, and a commitment to building God's kingdom on earth.

II. **There are three stages of transformation that occur to a follower of Jesus.**
   A. Spiritual rebirth: This happens at the moment of salvation.
   B. Soul renewal: This is a transforming process, brought about through our cooperation with the Holy Spirit and spending time in God's Word, in which we become more like Jesus.
   C. Bodily glorification: Our mortal bodies will one day be transformed to incorruptible bodies. Jesus' resurrected body serves as the prototype.

III. **The "catching away" is where believers meet Jesus in the air before His return.**
   A. Believers, dead and alive, will be caught up to meet Jesus at the trumpet's sound.
   B. The Greek word that Paul uses to describe this event (*harpazo*) describes a rapid, forceful, and sudden snatching away (1 Thessalonians 4:17).
   C. Another term used is *rapture*. This originates from *rapiemur*, the Latin translation of *harpazo*, which is related to the Latin word *raptus*, from which we get *rapture*.
   D. This event is distinct from the second coming, where Jesus physically returns to the Mount of Olives, and will happen before the outpouring of God's wrath.

IV. **This event is a source of encouragement, unity, and urgency for believers.**
   A. The "catching away" should inspire us to live passionately and avoid complacency.
   B. We are to focus on building God's kingdom and avoid complacency or procrastination.
   C. Our passion for Jesus—and our constant state of readiness for His return—are essential if we want to avoid being unprepared like the five unwise virgins (Matthew 25:1–13).

NOTES

DISCUSS | 35 MINUTES

Discuss what you just watched by answering the following questions.

1. Invite someone to read Luke 19:11–13. Notice that Jesus told this parable because "the people thought that the kingdom of God was going to appear at once." What does the king tell his ten servants to do while he is away? What do you think Jesus was saying to His followers about what they should be doing as they waited for God's kingdom to appear?

2. Read aloud 1 Corinthians 15:51–52. Paul reveals a "mystery" in this passage—something that was hidden to the Old Testament prophets and revealed to him by the Holy Spirit. What is this mystery? When will these events take place?

3. All believers in Christ will eventually undergo three transformations: (1) spiritual renewal (which occurs at salvation), (2) soul renewal (a lifelong process of growth), and (3) bodily glorification (which will occur at the last trumpet call). How do you see the second stage of transformation at work in your life right now? What hope does it give you to know that one day you will receive a resurrected and glorified body like Jesus had?

4. Christians have long held differing beliefs about when the church will be "caught up" to meet with Jesus in the air at the last trumpet sound—whether that is before, during, or after the tribulation. How can believers talk about these differences with humility and respect while still holding to the truth of what the Bible says about this event?

5. Invite someone to read Matthew 6:31–33. It is important for believers to not get embroiled in arguments about the "catching away" of the church and other minute details about the end times. What does Jesus say every believer's priority should be instead? What does He say will be "given" to those who choose to follow this instruction?

RESPOND | 10 MINUTES

The promise of Jesus' return isn't meant to spark debate but to stir devotion. It involves both mystery and hope—*mystery* in that we can't fully know everything that will happen when He returns, and *hope* in that we've been absolutely assured that He *is* coming again to make all things new. Take a few moments to reflect on this truth and then read the following passage.

> For the Lord himself will come down from heaven, with a loud command, with the voice of the archangel and with the trumpet call of God, and the dead in Christ will rise first. After that, we who are still alive and are left will be caught up together with them in the clouds to meet the Lord in the air. And so we will be with the Lord forever. Therefore encourage one another with these words.
>
> **1 THESSALONIANS 4:16-18**

What will happen first when the Lord Jesus comes down from heaven? What will happen "after that" to believers who are still alive on earth when the trumpet sounds?

Put yourself into this scene that Paul describes. What do you think you will feel when you see Jesus face-to-face? Excitement? Awe? Shock? How does imagining that moment change the way you want to live or prioritize things right now?

PRAY | 10 MINUTES

Thank the Lord for the hope of resurrection and for the promise that death will not have the final word over you. Ask Him to give you eyes to see beyond the temporary and to live with courage and compassion in light of eternity. Pray that your life would reflect a steady confidence in Jesus' return—not one marked by fear or debate but one marked by a faith that shows up in how you serve, speak, and love others.

SESSION FIVE

PERSONAL STUDY

You covered a lot of ground this week, so these personal studies will give you a chance to absorb the content in smaller pieces. You will see how the Bible paints a panoramic picture . . . from the resurrection of the dead, to the return of Christ, to the judgment of nations, to the marriage of the Lamb. It's a lot, but remember, you're not expected to decode every mystery! Think of it as standing on a high mountain where you can finally see the big picture. Take in the view. Let the Spirit highlight what He wants you to notice. And by the end, you will see that every prophecy, parable, and promise is pointing toward the same truth: Jesus is coming, and He is preparing His people to share His glory. As you work through these exercises, continue writing down your responses so you can share with your group next week. If you are reading *The King Is Coming*, first review chapters 14–21 of the book.

We will not all die,
but we will all be transformed!
It will happen in a moment,
in the blink of an eye, when the
last trumpet is blown.

1 CORINTHIANS 15:51–52 NLT

STUDY 1

BOTH GROOM AND KING

Every great love story has a moment of anticipation—the pause between promise and the fulfillment.

The return of Jesus sits in that sacred in-between. The Bible describes His coming as one grand event with two movements. First, Jesus returns to this world as the Bridegroom who comes for His bride. Second, Jesus returns to this earth as the King who comes to reign. The Bridegroom comes with intimacy and affection, receiving His beloved into safety. The King comes with power and justice, setting the world right. Together, these two movements reveal both His tenderness and His authority—two facets of the same love.

For those of us who belong to Christ, this isn't a day to dread but to desire. We are not appointed to wrath, as that judgment was absorbed at the cross when we accepted Jesus' offer of salvation. When Christ returns, it won't be to condemn His people but to complete what He began. He will draw His bride close before His righteous justice sweeps through the world.

Isaiah pictured this moment when he wrote, "Go, my people, enter your rooms and shut the doors behind you; hide yourselves for a little while until his wrath has passed by" (26:20). The world may shake. Nations may rise and fall. But the Bridegroom will not forget His own.

So when you feel the tension of waiting, remember who it is that you are waiting for. The One who came in humility will come again in glory. Until then, live like someone loved by a Bridegroom who delights in you and a King who defends you. Let that truth steady your hope.

1. Up to this point, we have primarily focused on Jesus returning as a Bridegroom to catch away His bride. Yet the Bible reveals that Jesus will also return as a conquering *King*. Look up each passage and write down what it says about Jesus being a sovereign King and Lord.

Passage	What this reveals about Jesus being sovereign King and Lord
Isaiah 9:6–7	
Daniel 7:13–14	
Zechariah 14:3–5	
Matthew 25:31–36	
Ephesians 1:18–21	
Hebrews 1:3–4	
Revelation 19:11–16	

2. Read 1 Thessalonians 5:8–10. For those who "belong to the day" (verse 8)—who have received salvation—Jesus' return is not a day to dread but a day to desire. What is the promise given in this verse for those who truly belong to Christ?

"God did not appoint us to wrath, but to obtain salvation through our Lord Jesus Christ. . . . Therefore comfort each other and edify one another, just as you also are doing" (1 Thessalonians 5:9, 11 NKJV). The bride (church) is not intended to experience the wrath of God, and Paul tells believers to *comfort* each other with these words. No one would consider the message of going through God's wrath as bringing comfort and encouragement. There are some who protest, "This is an *escape* mentality! We are appointed to tribulation." That is correct, as Jesus states, "In the world you will have tribulation" (John 16:33 NKJV). However, there is a huge difference between *tribulation* and *the tribulation*. Jesus is referencing persecutions, hardships, afflictions, and suffering from the trials and testings of this world.[30]

3. Read John 16:25–33. What reason does Jesus provide as to why He is giving this message to His disciples (see verse 28)? What is the difference between followers of Jesus being appointed to *tribulation* and those followers going through *the tribulation*?

4. Read Isaiah 26:20–21. When Noah entered the ark, God Himself shut the door behind him (see Genesis 7:16). How does that image of divine protection compare with Isaiah's picture of being hidden "for a little while" (26:20) until God's wrath has passed by?

The most important question to ask is: Where are these *chambers* for the resurrected dead in the Lord in Isaiah 26:20–21? Are they on earth or in heaven? In other words, as the indignation—the wrath of God—is being poured out, are God's people who are resurrected from the graves going to again live on earth and hide themselves in remote places such as forests, deserts, caves, communes, and so forth to avoid the plagues of judgments? No way! This thought is so far-fetched: dead people being resurrected so they can hide on earth from the persecution of the Antichrist and the wrath of God.

Now for the next important question: What happens in the same split second of these who are resurrected from the graves? The answer is found in the mystery that wasn't made known to Isaiah, or to any other Old Testament prophet, the mystery that Paul received "directly from the Lord." The mystery that those who are alive in Christ will also be caught up "together with them" (1 Thessalonians 4:17 NLT)—*in the same atomic second*—to meet the Lord and forever be with Him!

What is Scripture making clear? If the dead in the Lord are raised before the wrath is poured out (*hiding in chambers*), then the alive are also "caught up" before the wrath is poured out (*and will be in the same chambers*)! Both the dead and the living are united with the Lord within the same atomic second.[31]

5. When Paul describes believers in Christ being caught up "in the twinkling of an eye" (1 Corinthians 15:52), it's a breathtaking picture of unity and completion. There is now no separation between the living and the dead in Christ—no lag in God's timing. What does this reveal to you about God's precision and care in fulfilling His promises? How might remembering this moment help you face uncertainty or loss with greater peace?

STUDY 2

HOLDING THE LINE

Every passage that we have studied so far points to a consistent truth: *God has a plan, and He is not rushing or stalling in carrying out that plan*. Each prophetic event we have traced in Scripture moves toward the same promised moment: *Jesus returning for His bride*. But before that day arrives, another mystery unfolds—the mystery of restraint.

Paul wrote that a "secret power of lawlessness" (2 Thessalonians 2:7) is already at work in the world, but that a *restrainer* "now holds it back." This restrainer is the presence of God working through His church (see Matthew 16:18–19). Right now, every prayer we pray, every act of obedience we follow, and every choice we make to live differently pushes against the darkness trying to overtake the world. When we walk in light, we hold the line

Jesus said His return would come "as it was in the days of Noah" (Matthew 24:37). In Noah's time, people lived as if judgment would never come. They built, bought, and celebrated while the skies quietly gathered in warning. God waited until Noah and his family were safe in the ark before the flood began. That is prophecy fulfilled through mercy. God's heart always makes a way of escape before His justice is poured out.

You are living in that same tension. Mercy has been extended, the time is still open, but the hour is growing late. The Spirit within you still restrains evil around you. So hold your ground in truth, love, and holiness. As prophecy continues to unfold, let your life prove that God's delay is not neglect but mercy, giving one more chance for grace to be received.

1. On a scale of 1 to 10, how confident are you that your life is helping "hold the line" against the pull of darkness in today's world?

1 2 3 4 5 6 7 8 9 10

[not confident at all] [very confident]

What one area could you strengthen—whether through prayer, truth, or obedience—to live as a clearer reflection of Jesus where God has placed you?

2. The presence of God, working through His church, acts as a restraining force against evil. What will happen when that restrainer is removed? Look up the following passages and write down what the world looks like when godly people become scarce.

Passage	What the world looks like when godly people are scarce
Genesis 6:5–7	
Genesis 19:12–17	
Psalm 12:1–2	
Ezekiel 22:29–31	
Micah 7:2–3	

"I will build My church, and the gates of Hades shall not prevail against it" (Matthew 16:18 NKJV). . . . The church is to continuously advance. It's a force of light, and the gates of darkness cannot stop it. Just as darkness doesn't overcome light but is always overcome by light, even so the church has been not only a restraining force but an advancing force. In fact, Jesus clearly communicates in a parable that the church is to "occupy till I come" (Luke 19:13 KJV). . . . No force has been able to overcome it all through the two-thousand-year Age of Grace.[32]

3. Read Hebrews 10:28–31. God's love is beyond comprehension, but equally so is His wrath. What happens to those who trample on the grace of God? How does your fear of the Lord—your deep awe of God's holiness—impact what you tolerate in daily life?

4. Read Galatians 6:9 and 1 John 2:28. Where in your life do you feel weary from standing for what is right while the world moves the other way? What pressures make it hard for you to stay faithful and continue to stand for what is right?

"For you yourselves know perfectly that the day of the Lord [the seven-year tribulation] so comes as a thief in the night. For when they say, 'Peace and safety!' then sudden destruction comes upon them, as labor pains upon a pregnant woman. And they shall not escape. But you, brethren, are not in darkness, so that this Day should overtake you as a thief. You are all sons of light and sons of the day" (1 Thessalonians 5:2–5 NKJV).

Two things to note. First, unbelievers will all say, "Peace and safety." This will not be what people say as the seal, trumpet, and bowl judgments are being poured out. However, unbelievers could say this prior to the Bridegroom coming by stealth to catch away His bride. Second, Paul states this day will not overtake us as a thief because as *children of light*, we will have been caught away prior to the Day of the Lord—the outpouring of destruction. . . . This should create an urgency in your labor for His kingdom and move you to be prepared at all times.[33]

5. When you consider the terrible judgments that will take place during the seven-year tribulation, how does it compel you to live more awake and alert for Christ?

In what ways does considering these judgments create "an urgency in your labor" to promote the work of God's kingdom?

STUDY 3

PURE AND READY

In the book of Revelation, John writes of a great multitude proclaiming, "Let us rejoice and be glad and give him glory! For the wedding of the Lamb has come, and his bride has made herself ready. Fine linen, bright and clean, was given her to wear" (19:7–8). The wedding imagery isn't only about celebration but about preparation. A bride doesn't arrive at the altar by accident. Her readiness reflects love, attention, and honor to the one she's waited for.

In the same way, the purity of the church reflects our love, attention, and honor to Christ. God has already given you a spotless position, but He also calls you to live in a way that keeps your spiritual garment clean. Compromise can stain what grace has made white. When we excuse attitudes or actions that grieve the Spirit, we dull our spiritual senses and drift from intimacy with the One who purchased us at such a high cost.

Holiness isn't a narrow life; it's a wholehearted one. It's not about perfection but about devotion. It's about choosing what pleases Jesus because we love Him. The more we walk in His light, the more clearly we see the beauty of purity. The world may call it unnecessary, even old-fashioned, but heaven calls it the mark of the bride.

The same grace that saves you also empowers you to lead a pure life. When Jesus appears, those who have walked closely with Him will not shrink back in shame. Rather, they will rejoice, confident and ready for the joy set before them. The wedding *is* coming. So let every choice today reflect your love for the Bridegroom who is soon to appear.

1. The word *compromise* can be defined as "coming to agreement by mutual concession."[34] Compromise happens frequently in everyday life—but what happens when we try to compromise in our spiritual life? Look up the following passages and write down what each says about the dangers of believers in Christ compromising with the world.

Matthew 6:24: ____________________

____

Romans 12:2: ____________________

____

1 John 2:15: ____________________

____

2. Read 2 Corinthians 6:14–18. What attitudes or habits might God be asking you to "unyoke" when it comes to associating with the world? How would letting go of those things make room for deeper joy in your walk with Christ?

Consider a scenario in which the bride, in her big moment, appeared at the back of a church unkempt and wearing a soiled, filthy, and wrinkled white dress. The groom would be utterly shocked! His first thought would most likely be, *How inappropriate!* He would barely notice his bride because his attention would be fixated on the dirt, grime, and stains covering his bride's garment. He would be disappointed, to say the least, and perhaps angry. What would her lack of planning and inaction communicate to him? Was this just another event, was it insignificant, did she even care? It might be important to her in that moment, but her lack of preparation would reflect her overall view of the marriage; it would communicate a trivial attitude regarding the union.[35]

3. Think of this scenario of the bride with the stained wedding dress as you read Ephesians 4:22–24. What does it mean to "put off your old self" (the stained garment) and "put on the new self" (the pure garment) each day? How could the daily exercise of renewing your mind help you to resist compromise and keep your spiritual garment unstained?

4. Think about what your current level of spiritual preparation says about your relationship with Jesus, the Bridegroom. If you knew that the wedding were *tomorrow*, what three things would you do differently *today* to make yourself ready for the King?

♛ ______________________________

____

♛ ______________________________

____

When you pursue holiness, you live in communion with Jesus and thus will be confident at His return. However, if you flirt with darkness, you are pulled out of fellowship with Him and can easily stain your wedding garment. You will be ashamed by your garment stains at the grand reunion of the bride and Groom. When you understand the motive behind pursuing holiness, it becomes a delight, not a religious command. It's all dependent on your perspective, so chase after holiness. You will not be disappointed, and ten thousand years from now, you will not fret missing out on something. Instead, you will be forever glad you remained loyal to our heavenly Groom in this dark world.[36]

5. The author of Hebrews wrote, "Pursue peace with all people, *and holiness*, without which no one will see the Lord" (12:14 NKJV, emphasis added). What would you say is your primary motive for pursuing holiness? What are some of the benefits that you have personally experienced in your life because of your choice to chase after holiness?

CATCH UP AND CONNECT

Consider connecting with a fellow group member sometime this week to discuss some of your key insights from this session. Use any of the following prompts to help guide your discussion.

- Which truth from this week's study most strengthened your hope for Jesus' return? How did it help you see Jesus in a fuller way?
- The church is called to "hold the line" until the Bridegroom comes. Where do you feel God asking you to stay steady or shine brighter in a dark world?
- Holiness is more than obedience; it's devotion. What helps you keep your heart loyal to Jesus when distractions or compromise pull for your attention?
- God's plan is unfolding with precision. How does knowing that nothing in His timeline is delayed or random help you live with peace and confidence?
- As you have reflected this week on the return of the King, what has stirred in you the most? How will you respond to that feeling in the week ahead?

Use this time to go back and complete any of the study and reflection questions from previous days that you weren't able to finish. Make a note below of any revelations you've had and reflect on any growth or personal insights you've gained.

NEXT WEEK'S READING: Chapters 22–28 in *The King Is Coming*

WEEK 6 *at a glance*

THIS WEEK'S READING	Chapters 22–28 in *The King Is Coming*
GROUP MEETING	Read the Welcome and Open the group (page 112) Watch the video and take notes (pages 113–114) Discuss the questions that follow (page 115) Respond to the teaching and Pray (page 116)
PERSONAL STUDIES: STUDY 1 STUDY 2 STUDY 3	 "Stay Alert" (pages 119–122) "Keep Building" (pages 123–126) "The King Is Here" (pages 127–130)
WRAP UP	Connect with someone in your group Complete any unfinished studies (page 131)

SESSION SIX

HOW SHALL WE LIVE?

Let us hold unswervingly to the hope we profess, for he who promised is faithful.

HEBREWS 10:23

WELCOME | READ ON YOUR OWN

You're approaching the finish line. Over the past few weeks in *The King Is Coming*, you've walked through prophetic scenes that have stirred both awe and humility. You've been led by God as He has revealed His truth to you . . . layer by layer by layer. It's natural to feel the weight of everything you've covered. Biblical prophecy is not light reading but a mirror that exposes, refines, refocuses, purifies, and compels you to come closer to Jesus.

Throughout this study, you've seen the heart of a God who loves His church enough to correct it. This final session emphasizes that theme. Jesus speaks to you—as a member of His church—with honesty and affection, commending what is strong, confronting what is weak, and calling you back to your first love. He reminds you that zeal without love can harden into pride and that tolerance without truth can drift into deception. Both extremes leave the heart empty, and both can be healed only through repentance and renewed affection for Him.

Once again, the goal of prophecy (and this study) is to lead you into *readiness*. Your King is coming, and every act of quiet obedience and humble faithfulness will be revealed for what it truly is: precious, eternal, and accounted by Him. So, as you enter this final session, allow everything you've learned to settle in. And remember, the end of this story isn't just about future events. It's about you and your relationship with Jesus—your Bridegroom and King.

OPEN | 10 MINUTES

Get the session started by choosing one or both of the following questions to discuss together as a group:

- What is something that spoke to you in last week's personal study that you would like to share with the group?

  — *or* —

- Imagine your life as a movie trailer. What would the title be right now, and what theme would the narrator highlight?

WATCH | 25 MINUTES

Now watch the video for this session. Below is an outline of the key points covered during the teaching. Record any key concepts that stand out to you.

OUTLINE

I. **Believers are the bride of Christ and must live in holiness and readiness.**
   A. The wedding imagery used in Revelation 19:7–8 emphasizes that the bride has made herself ready. She is adorned in fine linen, representing righteous acts.
   B. This reveals that Jesus looks not only at what we *believe* but at what we *do*—our faith expressed through righteous works as empowered by His grace.
   C. The bride's preparation involves both external obedience and internal purity. Our motives and our intentions matter to God just as much as our actions.
   D. As believers in Christ, we are called to be set apart for Him (James 4:4).

II. **Holiness requires us to align our actions and motives with God.**
   A. *Justification* occurs at salvation, but *sanctification* is the ongoing process of us seeking to become more like Jesus each day.
   B. Paul urges us to "purify ourselves from everything that contaminates body and spirit" (2 Corinthians 7:1), which addresses both our actions and intentions.
   C. We must remember that our righteous acts are empowered by God's grace. We cannot produce works that are pleasing to God in our own strength.

III. **Jesus reveals His heart and His "secrets" to those who fear Him.**
   A. Holiness leads to a deeper and more personal relationship with Jesus.
   B. Friendship with Jesus is reserved for those who prioritize obedience and loyalty to Jesus over worldly desires (John 15:14).
   C. Intimacy with Jesus allows us to hear His whispers and receive His revelation.
   D. Pursuing holiness will ensure that we are ready for our Bridegroom's return.

IV. **Finishing well for Christ means living with eternity in view.**
   A. The parable of the ten virgins in Matthew 25:1–13 warns us against holding back any part of our lives from God. We are urged to be fully devoted to Jesus.
   B. Every prophetic word about Jesus' coming is meant to refine our hearts, calling us to holiness that flows from love and confident expectation.
   C. Prophecy reorders our priorities. We invest in what will last, endure difficulty with perspective, and find strength in knowing how the story ends.
   D. The prophetic promise of Jesus' return invites us to live ready and radiant, shaping our daily choices around the reality that the King is coming soon.

NOTES

DISCUSS | 35 MINUTES

Discuss what you just watched by answering the following questions.

1. Invite someone to read Revelation 19:7–8. Imagine a bride showing up on her wedding day wearing an unkempt and stained gown. What would that communicate to her groom? In the same way, what does it communicate to Jesus (the Bridegroom) when those in the church (His bride) live in an unrighteous and worldly way as they wait for Him?

2. The picture of the bride who has "made herself ready" (verse 7) is one of both internal purity *and* external obedience to the Lord. Walk through a typical week. What is one practice to start, one to stop, and one to continue doing that would reflect real readiness?

3. Holiness is not *legalism* but the doorway to *intimacy* with God. How does seeing holiness in that way challenge or reshape the way you have thought about it in the past?

4. Read John 15:14–16. How does Jesus define the person whom He considers to be His "friend"? What special blessing does this friend of Jesus receive?

5. Invite someone to read Hebrews 12:14 and James 4:4. What does it means to "see the Lord" in everyday life—not just someday in heaven but in the here and now? How would you define what it means to have "friendship with the world"? What does it look like to stay engaged in culture without being influenced by it to live an unholy life?

RESPOND | 10 MINUTES

The promise of Jesus' return is a call for you to live differently—to lead a holy or "set apart" life. When you keep your heart loyal to your Bridegroom, the waiting becomes worship and the preparation becomes joy. Take a few minutes to read the passage below and reflect on what it means to stay ready.

> But in keeping with his promise we are looking forward to a new heaven and a new earth, where righteousness dwells. So then, dear friends, since you are looking forward to this, make every effort to be found spotless, blameless and at peace with him.
>
> **2 PETER 3:13–14**

Peter connects readiness with peace. What helps you remain spiritually alert without growing anxious or weary as you wait for Jesus to return?

How does this passage reshape the way you think about waiting? What does diligence look like when it is fueled by love for Christ rather than pressure to perform?

PRAY | 10 MINUTES

Take a few minutes to close this study in gratitude and surrender. Thank God for walking with you through each session, for revealing truth as you were ready to receive it, and for using His Word to stir your heart toward readiness. Ask the Holy Spirit to help you live alert, pure, and steadfast in love until the day you see Jesus face-to-face. Invite Him to refine your motives, steady your heart, and strengthen your faith in the waiting. Finally, ask God to help each of you continue walking in unity as you encourage each other to lead faithful and holy lives.

SESSION SIX

PERSONAL STUDY

You've come to the end of this study . . . but really, you've just scratched the surface when it comes to what is revealed in Scripture about the return of Jesus the King. Over the past six weeks, you have traced God's plan from His covenants to Jesus' return and seen how prophecy calls you to live in readiness, purity, and steadfastness for Christ. In this final personal study section, you will dive deeper into exploring how to guard against spiritual "drift" in a culture filled with distraction, how endurance and patient faith prepare you for the outpouring of God's Spirit, and how living with eternity in view transforms what you value and how you serve. As you work through these exercises, continue to write down your responses. If you are reading *The King Is Coming* alongside this study, first review chapters 22–28 of the book.

*"Be dressed for service
and keep your lamps burning,
as though you were waiting
for your master to return
from the wedding feast."*

LUKE 12:35–36 NLT

STUDY 1

STAY ALERT

It is sobering to realize that Jesus' messages to the churches in Revelation 2–3 weren't delivered to skeptics. They were given to believers who had once burned brightly for Jesus but since had drifted. This type of drift rarely happens overnight. It starts with small compromises . . . a little less time in prayer, a little more comfort, a few compromises in integrity.

Jesus' message to each of the seven churches in Revelation was the same at its core: *Stay alert*. Don't assume that good intentions or religious activity can replace a living relationship with Him. Don't lose sight of Him in the midst of the world's noise.

What does staying alert look like for the church today? It's as simple, and as difficult, as keeping short accounts with God. It's choosing repentance over rationalization when the Spirit convicts. It's guarding our hearts when distraction or comfort starts to dull our hunger for Him. It's not about perfection but about responsiveness.

Jesus instructed, "Go back to what you heard and believed at first; hold to it firmly" (Revelation 3:3 NLT). In other words, remember what first moved you to follow Him and make space for that kind of devotion again. If you sense your heart cooling or your passion fading, you don't have to stay there. Ask God to reignite your love for Him. He is faithful to breathe fresh strength into hearts that want to return to Him.

The goal isn't to live in fear of losing ground. It's to walk in renewed love for the One who never stopped pursuing you. Staying alert isn't about pressure but about presence. It's living responsive, with your eyes fixed on Jesus, until the day He returns.

1. Jesus' messages to the seven churches in Revelation 2–3 was to "alert" them of certain aspects of their faith that needed correcting. Imagine your faith had a notifications setting. What kind of alert would God need to send you most often? (Circle the one that best fits.)

- A gentle reminder to slow down
- A warning that distraction is creeping in
- An invitation to reconnect after too much silence
- A nudge to pause everything for a while and simply rest in His presence

2. Read Revelation 2:1–7. Jesus opens this letter to the church in Ephesus by saying, "I know your deeds" (verse 2). Write out what Jesus says He appreciates about this church.

verse 2	"your ____ _____ and your _______________"
verse 2	"you cannot _________ _________ __________"
verse 2	"you have _______ those who _______ __ __ __________ but are not"
verse 3	"you have _____________"
verse 3	"and have ___________ ___________ for ___ ______"
verse 3	"and have not ______ _________"

Jesus then says, "But I have this complaint against you. You don't love me or each other as you did at first!" (Revelation 2:4 NLT). What are some traits of a believer who has left his or her first love for Jesus and others? How do you prevent this from happening in your life?

> "To the angel of the church in Smyrna . . . I know your afflictions and your poverty" (Revelation 2:8–9). Again, Jesus opens with this church's works—what they do rather than what they believe. He states His full awareness of the tribulation or persecution they're enduring. Also, that they are poor, but He is quick to add that they are really rich. . . . The Smyrna church didn't receive any correction from the Master, only instructions for handling what they were up against and what was coming. He recognized how looked down upon they were by those who claimed to be in covenant relationship with God but were really a part of the congregation of Satan. Jesus warned they would be sorely persecuted, even thrown into prison.[37]

3. Read Revelation 2:8–11. What instructions does Jesus give to the church in Smyrna about how to handle what they are up against and what was coming?

4. Read Revelation 2:12–17. Jesus opens this letter to the church in Pergamum by saying, "I know your works" (verse 13 NKJV). What two things does Jesus commend them for doing?

verse 13 "you ________ ______ to my ________"

verse 13 "you did not ___________ your _______ in _____"

Jesus then says, "Nevertheless, I have a few things against you" (verse 14). What was the church in Pergamum tolerating? What was Jesus' warning if the people did not repent?

Thyatira was the smallest of the cities to receive a direct message from Jesus. . . . His complaint [against them] is stern, and so important to emphasize. His rebukes don't center around their actions but rather their *inactions*. They were tolerating practices that were destroying people's spiritual lives. . . . In Thyatira's case it was a woman whom He compares to Jezebel of the Old Testament. "But I have this complaint against you. You are *permitting* that woman—that Jezebel who calls herself a prophet—to lead my servants astray. She teaches them to commit sexual sin and to eat food offered to idols" (Revelation 2:20 NLT, emphasis added).

"Jezebel" operated under the motive of subtly pulling people away from devotion and faithfulness to God and wooing them over to what the world chases after. The key word for this church is *permitting*, which is synonymous with *tolerating*. The church was overlooking what should be confronted.

In essence, *silence is nonverbal communication*. By not saying a word, it conveys agreement and grants permission by communicating, "What you're doing is fine." There is an old Latin proverb that states, "Silence gives consent; he ought to have spoken when he was able to." It's clear this church leader's sin was not what they were doing or saying but what they were *not doing* and *not saying*.[38]

5. Read Jesus' words to the church in Thyatira in Revelation 2:18–29. When is silence wise? When does it become a compromise?

Think about an area (whether in faith, relationships, or culture) where you have stayed quiet even though conviction stirred. What would it look like to speak truth with courage in that area instead of allowing tolerance to feel like peace?

STUDY 2

KEEP BUILDING

Readiness isn't passive. It's active faithfulness. Jesus said, "Be dressed ready for service and keep your lamps burning" (Luke 12:35). Those words aren't just for pastors or missionaries; they're for everyone who follows Him. Every believer has been entrusted with a portion of His work. Some serve in homes, some in classrooms or hospitals, some in offices or neighborhoods, but all are called to reflect His image and domain in their corner of the world.

God designed us with purpose long before we were born. Paul wrote, "For we are God's handiwork, created in Christ Jesus to do good works, which God prepared in advance for us to do" (Ephesians 2:10). Those works might seem ordinary, but when offered to God, they are powerful. The problem is that distractions make it easy for us to stop building. We lose confidence, compare ourselves to others, and wonder if what we're doing really matters. All the while, Scripture reminds us that faithfulness in small things has great reward.

When God's people were exiled to Babylon, the Lord spoke through Jeremiah and told them to "build houses," "plant gardens," and "seek the peace and prosperity of the city" where they lived (Jeremiah 29:5, 7). Even in a foreign land, they were to work for the good of others. This same instruction applies to Christians. Wherever God has placed you—even in environments that feel resistant or indifferent to His truth—He calls you to stay faithful, to build, and to bless.

Your calling isn't measured by applause but by obedience. So keep showing up. Keep building what God has assigned you to build. Seek the good of the place you've been planted, because, even there, God's purposes are unfolding.

1. On a scale of 1 to 10, how faithful do you feel in staying engaged where God has placed you—even when the results seem slow or unnoticed?

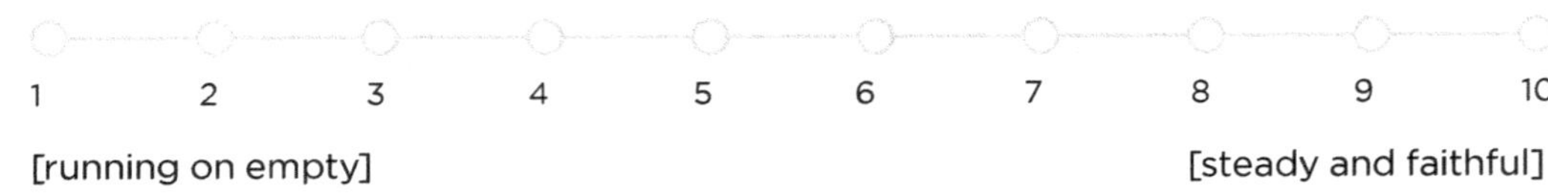

1 2 3 4 5 6 7 8 9 10

[running on empty] [steady and faithful]

What might help you take one step toward serving with endurance and joy, trusting that your obedience to God still matters in the times of waiting?

2. Read Revelation 3:1–6. Jesus opens His letter to the church in Sardis by stating, "I know your deeds" (verse 1). What does Jesus go on to say about their deeds? What is His warning if the people in the church do not "wake up" (verse 3)?

What Jesus says to Philadelphia He says to any others who heed His correction and endure in obedience: "Because you have obeyed my command to persevere, I will protect you from the great time of testing that will come upon the whole world to test those who belong to this world" (Revelation 3:10 NLT). It appears from Jesus' words and other portions of Scripture that all loyal believers will be caught up before the seven-year tribulation. However, not all who classify themselves as believers are necessarily true Christ followers. . . . It's easy to surrender all to Him but so difficult if you're still enamored with this world. God will give you the grace if your heart is sincere. Your opportunity is right now if you haven't totally surrendered your life to His lordship. It's not too late, and a wonderful life awaits you![39]

3. Read Revelation 3:7–13. Jesus opens this letter by also stating, "I know your deeds" (verse 8). What two things does Jesus commend them for doing?

verse 8 "you have kept ___ ________"

verse 8 "and have not denied ___ _______"

Jesus tells the church in Philadelphia, "I am coming soon" (verse 11). What does He want them to "hold on to" and keep building in the meantime?

How does this apply to believers in Christ today?

4. Read Revelation 3:14–22. Jesus also says to this church, "I know your deeds," and then adds, "you are neither cold nor hot" (verse 15). What does it mean to be *lukewarm* in your faith? What foundation had the people in this church built their lives on?

"You saw me before I was born. Every day of my life was recorded in your book. Every moment was laid out before a single day had passed" (Psalm 139:16 NLT). Your assigned "good works" were prepared prior to your birth. . . . God wrote your intended magnificent biography before your parents ever knew you. In essence, you were created on purpose for a purpose. When you hear the statement, "He (or she) has a calling on his (or her) life," does your mind go to the limited few—a pastor, worship leader, missionary, or other full-time vocational ministry position? If so, this is far from the full picture. Every child of God has a calling. It may be in the realm of education, health care, government, the arts, the marketplace . . . The possibilities are too numerous to list.[40]

5. Read Colossians 3:23–24. *You* have a calling on your life. How does Paul advise you to treat all the tasks that you do? How could the perspective you are working "for the Lord, not for human masters" insert new purpose into what feels routine or overlooked?

STUDY 3

THE KING IS HERE

Prophecy can feel weighty, but remember: *It's not meant to create dread.* Prophecy is meant to strengthen your faith. Every vision, symbol, and promise is God's way of saying, "I am faithful to finish what I began." He has a plan for the world, for His people, and for you.

One day, you will stand before the judgment seat of Christ. If you are a follower of Jesus, this moment won't bring condemnation but celebration. Your sins were already judged at the cross, so what awaits you is evaluation and reward. This judgment will include the unveiling of how you lived, loved, and served in Jesus' name. Paul wrote that your work "will be revealed with fire, and the fire will test the quality of each person's work. If what has been built survives, the builder will receive a reward" (1 Corinthians 3:13–14).

Every small act of obedience will matter. Every hidden kindness and sacrifice, every unseen moment of prayer, every choice to love when it was costly . . . Jesus will remember it all. He promised, "Look, I am coming soon! My reward is with me" (Revelation 22:12).

But as you look forward to that day, remember this important truth: *The King who is coming is also the King who is here.* He hasn't left you to endure alone. His final promise before ascending still stands: "Surely I am with you always, to the very end of the age" (Matthew 28:20). The same Presence who will one day fill eternity already fills your everyday reality.

So live ready, but not restless. Serve faithfully, knowing He walks beside you now. Yes, the King is coming, but He is also already here.

1. Paul writes, "He who began a good work in you will carry it on to completion until the day of Christ Jesus" (Philippians 1:6). How does that bring you confidence today? How does knowing that Jesus is coming again *and* still working in you bring peace to your waiting?

2. Read John 14:18 and Hebrews 13:5. *The King who is coming is also the King who is here.* How is Jesus making His presence known to you today?

We live in a time when the virtue of patience is waning. It's hard to stay steady and consistent over long periods of time when we've been conditioned to instantaneous or quick results. It's not just one aspect of our lives but nearly all areas. Whether it's information, entertainment, food, education, purchases, loans, or the countless other areas of life that have been condensed, what once required much more time to obtain now takes just moments. Many innovations have fabulously improved our quality of life, but the danger arises when "instantaneous results" bleed over into what needs consistency over time to obtain. One of these important qualities is the development of inner strength to *endure until the end* (see Matthew 10:22; 24:13; Mark 13:13).[41]

---

3. Read Galatians 6:9. Where are you most tempted to give up or "become weary" in doing good—whether that is in ministry, in prayer, or in serving others? How do you need Jesus, the King, to make His presence known to you so that you can persevere?

The greatest award ceremony of all time is rapidly approaching for believers. There are many eternal prizes that will be handed out. The rewards will be much more than medals, plaques, or trophies; they will be accompanied by eternal positions that carry responsibility and authority. This event is referred to as the judgment seat of Christ. Paul urges a very carnal church [in 1 Corinthians 9:24–26] to wake up so they don't have regrets at this ceremony. He urges them, as well as us, to diligently train and run with purpose in every step in order to receive the everlasting prize. We are told to win; however, we're not competing against each other, rather against a world that's bent on hindering or even stopping us. We all should be cheering for each other![42]

---

4. Read 1 Corinthians 9:24–26. Picture the moment you and Jesus sit down together after the race is over—not in a grand ceremony but in a personal conversation. What moments might He encourage you to see differently—not with shame but through His grace? If He were to replay scenes from your life on a

screen, what moments do you think He would pause on and smile? Take a moment to write some of these down or draw one below.

5. Paul, after counseling the believers in Thessalonica on how to stay awake and sober as they awaited Jesus' return, gave them this instruction: "Therefore encourage one another and build each other up, just as in fact you are doing" (1 Thessalonians 5:11). We are told to run the race of faith to win—but we are not competing against each other. As you close this study, what is one practical way you will cheer on another believer in Christ to run his or her race well? How can you encourage that person with what you've learned in this study?

WRAP UP

Consider connecting with a group member to talk about some of the insights from this final session. Use any of the prompts below to guide your discussion.

- What part of this study most changed how you see Jesus: His character, His patience, or His authority as King? Why did that stand out?
- Prophecy reveals both God's precision and His mercy. How has understanding the bigger picture of His plan deepened your trust in His timing?
- Holiness and endurance go hand in hand. When was a time that staying faithful (especially when it wasn't easy) helped strengthen your love for God?
- Jesus isn't only the coming *King* but also the present *Lord* who walks with us now. Where have you sensed His nearness in a new way this week?
- As you move forward, what is one truth from this study you want to make sure you grasp and live out in your daily life—something that will keep you steady, hopeful, and ready until the King returns?

Use this time to go back and complete any of the personal study and reflection questions from previous days that you weren't able to finish. Make a note of what God has revealed to you. Finally, talk with your group about what study you may want to go through next. Put a date on the calendar for when you'll meet next to study God's Word and dive deeper into community.

LEADER'S GUIDE

Thank you for leading your group through this study! What you have chosen to do is valuable and will make a difference in their lives. *The King Is Coming* is a six-session study built around video content and small-group interaction. As the group leader, imagine yourself as the host of a party. Your job is to take care of your guests by managing the details so that when your guests arrive, they can focus on one another and on the interaction around the topic for that session.

Your role as the group leader is not to answer all the questions or reteach the content—the video, book, and study guide will do most of that work. Rather, your job is to guide the experience and cultivate your small group into a connected and engaged community. This will make it a place for your group members to process, question, and reflect on all that they have learned. There are several elements in this leader's guide that will help you as you structure your study and reflection time, so be sure to follow along and take advantage of each one.

BEFORE YOU BEGIN

Before your first meeting, make sure the group members have a copy of this study guide. Alternately, you can hand out the study guides at your first meeting and give the members some time to look over the material and ask any preliminary questions. Also, make sure the group members are aware they have access to the streaming videos at any time by following the instructions provided with this guide. During your first meeting, ask the members to provide their names, phone numbers, and email addresses so that you can keep in touch.

Generally, the ideal size for a group is eight to ten people, which will ensure that everyone has enough time to participate in discussions. If you have more people, you might want to break up the main group into smaller subgroups. Encourage those who show up at the first meeting to commit to attending the duration of the study, as this will help the group members get to know one another, create stability for the group, and help you know how best to prepare to lead the participants through the material.

Each session begins with an opening reflection in the Welcome section. The questions that follow in the Open section serve as icebreakers to get the group members thinking about the topic. In the rest of the study, it is generally not a good idea to have everyone answer every question—a free-flowing discussion is more desirable. But with the icebreaker questions, you can go around the circle and ask each person to respond. Encourage shy people to share, but don't force them.

At your first meeting, let the group members know that each session contains a personal study section they can use to continue to engage with the content until the next meeting. While doing this section is optional, it will help cement the concepts presented during the group study time so they can better apply what they have learned about Jesus' return.

Let them know that if they choose to do so, they can watch the video for the next session by accessing the streaming code provided with this study guide. Invite them to bring any questions and insights to your next meeting, especially if they had a breakthrough moment or didn't understand something.

PREPARATION FOR EACH SESSION

As the leader of your group, there are a few things you should do to best prepare for each meeting:

- **Read through the session.** This will help you become more familiar with the content and know how to structure the discussion times.
- **Decide how the videos will be used.** Determine whether you want the members to watch the videos ahead of time (again, via the streaming access code provided with this study guide) or together as a group.
- **Decide which questions you want to discuss.** Based on the length of your group discussions, you may not be able to get through all the questions. So look over the discussion questions provided in each session and mark which ones you definitely want to cover.

- **Be familiar with the questions you want to discuss.** When the group meets, you will be watching the clock, so make sure you are familiar with the questions you have selected.
- **Pray for your group.** Pray for your group members and ask God to lead them as they study His Word and listen to the Holy Spirit.

In many cases, there will be no one "right" answer to the questions. Answers will vary, especially when the group members are sharing their personal experiences.

STRUCTURING THE DISCUSSION TIME

You will need to determine with your group how long you want your meetings to last so that you can plan your time accordingly. Suggested times for each section have been provided in this study guide, and if you adhere to these times, your group will meet for ninety minutes. However, many groups like to meet for two hours. If this describes your particular group, follow the times listed in the right-hand column of the chart given below.

Section	90 Minutes	120 Minutes
OPEN (discuss one or more of the opening questions for the session)	15 minutes	20 minutes
WATCH (watch the teaching material together and take notes)	20 minutes	20 minutes
DISCUSS (discuss the study questions you selected ahead of time)	35 minutes	50 minutes
RESPOND (write down takeaways)	10 minutes	15 minutes
PRAY (pray together and dismiss)	10 minutes	15 minutes

As the group leader, it is up to you to keep track of the time and to keep things on schedule. You might want to set a timer for each segment so that both you and the group members know when the time is up. (There are some good phone apps for timers that play a gentle chime or other pleasant sound instead of a disruptive noise.)

Don't be concerned if group members are quiet or slow to share. People are often quiet when they are pulling together their ideas, and this might be a new experience for some of them. Just ask a question and let it hang in the air until someone shares. You can then say, "Thank you. What about others? What came to you when you watched that portion of the teaching?"

GROUP DYNAMICS

Leading a group through *The King Is Coming* will prove to be highly rewarding both to you and your group members. But you still may encounter challenges along the way! Discussions can get off track. Group members may not be sensitive to the needs and ideas of others. Some might worry that they will be expected to talk about matters that make them feel awkward. Others may express comments that result in disagreements.

To help ease this strain on you and the group, consider the following ground rules:

- When someone raises a question or comment that is off the main topic, suggest you deal with it another time, or, if you feel led to go in that direction, let the group know that you will be spending some time discussing it.
- If someone asks a question that you don't know how to answer, admit it and move on. At your discretion, feel free to invite group members to comment on questions that call for personal experience.
- If you find that one or two people are dominating the discussion time, direct a few questions to others in the group. Outside the main group time, ask the more dominating members to help you draw out the quieter ones. Work to make them part of the solution instead of part of the problem.
- When a disagreement occurs, encourage the group members to process the matter in love. Encourage those on opposite sides to restate what they heard the other side say about the matter, and then invite each side to evaluate if that perception is accurate. Lead the group in examining other passages related to the topic and look for common ground.

When any of these issues arise, encourage your group members to follow these words from Scripture: "Love one another" (John 13:34); "If possible, so far as it depends on you, be at peace with all people" (Romans 12:18); "Whatever is true . . . honorable . . . right . . . pure . . . lovely . . . commendable . . . if there is any excellence and if anything worthy of praise, think about these things" (Philippians 4:8); and, "Everyone must be quick to hear, slow to speak, and slow to anger" (James 1:19). This will make your group time more rewarding and beneficial for everyone who attends.

Thank you for leading your group. You are making a difference in your members' lives and having an impact as they anticipate the coming of the King.

NOTES

1. John Bevere, *The King Is Coming: It's Time to Prepare for the Return of Christ* (W Publishing, 2026), chapter 1.
2. Bevere, *The King Is Coming*, chapter 1.
3. Spiros Zodhiates, *The Complete Word Study Dictionary: New Testament* (AMG Publishers, 2000).
4. Johannes P. Louw and Eugene Albert Nida, *Greek-English Lexicon of the New Testament: Based on Semantic Domains* (United Bible Societies, 1996), 532.
5. Bevere, *The King Is Coming*, chapter 2.
6. Bevere, *The King Is Coming*, chapter 2.
7. Bevere, *The King Is Coming*, chapter 3.
8. Bevere, *The King Is Coming*, chapter 3.
9. Bevere, *The King Is Coming*, chapter 5.
10. Bevere, *The King Is Coming*, chapter 5.
11. Bevere, *The King Is Coming*, chapter 6.
12. Bevere, *The King Is Coming*, chapter 6.
13. "Shared Pain Brings People Together," Association for Psychological Science, September 9, 2014, https://www.psychologicalscience.org/news/releases/shared-pain-brings-people-together.html.
14. Bevere, *The King Is Coming*, chapter 7.
15. Bevere, *The King Is Coming*, chapter 7.
16. Bevere, *The King Is Coming*, chapter 8.
17. Bevere, *The King Is Coming*, chapter 8.
18. Bevere, *The King Is Coming*, chapter 10 (adapted).
19. Bevere, *The King Is Coming*, chapter 10.
20. Bevere, *The King Is Coming*, chapter 10.
21. Cyprian of Carthage, *On the Unity of the Church*, § 26, in *The Treatises of Cyprian* (c. AD 251), https://www.newadvent.org/fathers/050701.htm.
22. Bevere, *The King Is Coming*, chapter 10.
23. Bevere, *The King Is Coming*, chapter 11.
24. Bevere, *The King Is Coming*, chapter 11.
25. Bevere, *The King Is Coming*, chapter 12.
26. Bevere, *The King Is Coming*, chapter 12.
27. Bevere, *The King Is Coming*, chapter 13.
28. Louw and Nida, *Greek-English Lexicon of the New Testament: Based on Semantic Domains*, 352.
29. Bevere, *The King Is Coming*, chapter 13.
30. Bevere, *The King Is Coming*, chapter 15.
31. Bevere, *The King Is Coming*, chapter 16.

32. Bevere, *The King Is Coming*, chapter 17.
33. Bevere, *The King Is Coming*, chapter 18.
34. *Merriam-Webster*, s.v. "compromise," https://www.merriam-webster.com/dictionary/compromise.
35. Bevere, *The King Is Coming*, chapter 20.
36. Bevere, *The King Is Coming*, chapter 21.
37. Bevere, *The King Is Coming*, chapter 22.
38. Bevere, *The King Is Coming*, chapter 23 (adapted).
39. Bevere, *The King Is Coming*, chapter 25.
40. Bevere, *The King Is Coming*, chapter 25.
41. Bevere, *The King Is Coming*, chapter 26.
42. Bevere, *The King Is Coming*, chapter 27.
43. Bevere, *The King Is Coming*, chapter 28.

ABOUT
JOHN BEVERE

John Bevere is an international minister, bestselling author, and co-founder of Messenger International—a ministry dedicated to developing uncompromising followers of Christ who transform their world. For more than forty years, John has carried a passion to see believers walk in holy awe, living out their faith with purpose and conviction.

Known for his bold, uncompromising approach to God's Word, John has written 25 books that have sold millions of copies and been translated into more than 150 languages. Through Messenger International, John and his wife Lisa have equipped the global Church by distributing over 70 million resources across 240 nations. Their revolutionary MessengerX app provides free digital discipleship resources in over 120 languages, currently reaching users in more than 30,000 cities worldwide.

John hosts "The John Bevere Podcast," where he shares timeless truths for changing times, helping believers live empowered and prepared. His ability to communicate challenging biblical concepts with clarity and conviction has made him a sought-after speaker at conferences and churches globally.

When John is home in Franklin, Tennessee, and not crafting his next message, you'll find him on the pickleball court holding his own against his four sons, loving on his grandchildren, or trying to convince Lisa to take up golf.

OTHER BOOKS BY JOHN BEVERE

A Heart Ablaze
The Awe of God*
The Bait of Satan*
Breaking Intimidation*
Called*
Drawing Near*
Driven by Eternity*
Enemy Access Denied
Everyday Courage*
Extraordinary*
The Fear of the Lord*
God, Where Are You?!*
Good or God?*
The Holy Spirit: An Introduction*
Honor's Reward*
How to Respond When You Feel Mistreated
Killing Kryptonite*
Relentless*
Rescued
The Story of Marriage*
Thus Saith the Lord?
Under Cover*
The Voice of One Crying
X: Multiply Your God-Given Potential*

POPULAR BOOKS BY LISA BEVERE

Adamant*
Girls with Swords*
Lioness Arising*
The Fight for Female*
Without Rival*

---

*Also available as a course

If this message impacted you, consider leading a group study to bring others along your journey!

Find the group video study, bulk ordering discounts, and more at:

johnbevere.com/thekingiscoming

The John Bevere Podcast

WATCH ON YOUTUBE:

LISTEN ON:

 Apple Podcasts

 Spotify

 Google Play

CONNECT WITH JOHN:

 Instagram

 Facebook

 TikTok

 X (formerly Twitter)

johnbevere.com

From the Publisher

GREAT STUDIES

ARE EVEN BETTER WHEN THEY'RE SHARED!

Help others find this study:

- Post a review at your favorite online bookseller.
- Post a picture on a social media account and share why you enjoyed it.
- Send a note to a friend who would also love it—or, better yet, go through it with them!

Thanks for helping others grow their faith!

www.ingramcontent.com/pod-product-compliance
Lightning Source LLC
LaVergne TN
LVHW060953150726
843125LV00003B/4

* 9 7 8 0 3 1 0 1 7 9 4 6 7 *